HEAD ON FIRE

A BLACK HAIR MEMOIR
ON LOSS AND HEALING

Published in the United States of America

Silent Books Publishing, Baltimore, MD
This book was produced in partnership with Silent Books
Publishing, a full-service self-publishing company helping
authors bring their stories to life.
silentbookspublishing.com

This is a work of nonfiction. Some names and identifying
details have been changed to protect the privacy of individuals.

This memoir reflects the author's personal experiences and
is not intended as medical or psychological advice. Readers
should seek qualified professional support for any health or
mental health concerns.

ISBN: 979-8-9911861-4-8 (Paperback)

Book design by Jessica Do
Illustrations by Maya L. Johnson and Jessica Do
Author photo by Zhee Chatmon

Printed in the United States of America
2025

HEAD ON FIRE

A BLACK HAIR MEMOIR
ON LOSS AND HEALING

By Maya L. Johnson

Memoirs help us understand the life
experiences of another like mirrors,
which help us see ourselves anew.

———

Silent Books Publishing,
Baltimore, MD

For Sydney

CONTENTS

When I think of my hair, I think of cotton.
Like cotton, my hair has two facets.
On the one hand, there's beauty,
abundance, ease, and softness;
on the other, racism, absorption of
racial trauma, and physical pain.

COTTON

———

C otton, of the genus *Gossypium* and family *Malvaceae*, is a unique and beautiful plant. Its leaves are broad, its flowers delicate, and the bolls soft and dense. Everywhere cotton can grow, it grows plentifully, and its gentle and absorptive nature makes it one of the most revered crops across the globe.

Here in the U.S., cotton is also emblematic of racism. From 1619, when a ship called the *White Lion* arrived at Port Comfort in Virginia[1] through the mid-nineteenth century, more than 360,000 people were coerced from their homes in Africa and brought to the U.S. mainland[2] to pick cotton (among other crops), building wealth and prosperity for white European colonizers. That shocking number is not exact since the data gathered in the Trans-Atlantic Slave Trade Database isn't complete. In any case, it represents a tiny portion of the more than 12.5 million Africans subjugated to the trans-Atlantic slave trade.[3] In 1860, just before the Civil War, there were nearly 4 million enslaved people with a market value of $3.5 billion[4] — equivalent to $136 trillion today[5] — living in the U.S.

The tremendous wealth of white enslavers and their descendants came at the direct and painful expense

---

[1] *The New York Times.* "The 1619 Project." August 14, 2019.
[2] "Trans-Atlantic Slave Trade - Database." Accessed April 17, 2023. https://www.slavevoyages.org/voyage/database.
[3] *The New York Times.* "The 1619 Project."
[4] "The Civil War and Reconstruction Era, 1845-1877 | Open Yale Courses." Spring 2008. https://oyc.yale.edu/history/hist-119.
[5] "$3,500,000,000 in 1860 → 2025 | Inflation Calculator." Accessed September 19, 2025. https://www.in2013dollars.com/us/inflation/1860?amount=3500000000.

of kidnapped Africans and the enslaved generations who followed them, all of whom were subjected to forced labor, forced breeding, whipping, mutilation, torture, and rape, among other crimes against humanity. The violence, cruelty, exploitation, and indignities enslaved people faced were unrelenting. And the racism used as justification for enslaving Black people for hundreds of years and the resulting brutalization of Black bodies strongly persists to this day — in both minds and institutions.

Even so, for as much as cotton exemplifies racism, it's also a powerful symbol of resistance. Enslaved women used the root as contraception and a tool for miscarriage or abortion to prevent giving birth to babies resulting from rape by enslavers or forced intercourse with other slaves, who'd be born into slavery. This was an act of willful defiance and an unstoppable way of disrupting the "self-generating workforce"[6] enslavers were intent on sustaining.

I first saw a cotton plant on television when I watched the original miniseries *Roots* at the impressionable age of 7. At no point since then could I look at a cotton plant and not think about the astonishing savagery, sadism, and wickedness of slavery — that is, until I saw a real cotton plant at a Juneteenth celebration when I was 50. That was the moment the plant took on new meaning. Now, when I see cotton I'm reminded of the immense courage, strength, resourcefulness, perseverance, grit, determination, and resolve of Black enslaved people to endure and survive, coupled with their resistance to oppression in every way they could.

---

[6] Dadzie, Stella Abasa. *A Kick in the Belly: Women, Slavery and Resistance.* Verso Books, 2020.

Throughout my years of living and learning, I've also seen how cotton resembles my hair: the discrimination, harassment, microaggressions, and microassaults I've witnessed and been the target of; my journey from self-loathing to love and acceptance of everything that's unique and beautiful about my hair; and the pain, breakthroughs, and revelations of losing it.

INTRODUCTION

———

What you're holding is the story of my hair and my hair loss journey. Much like cotton in the American South, it's a story of discovery, trauma, and renewal.

When I started wearing a TWA (teeny weeny afro) — the most effortless style for me to maintain — for the second time in my life, I would catch the hair I shed after washing between my fingers, roll it into a ball, and rub it along my face as if it were cotton. Like cotton, the texture of my loose, natural hair is easy to shape and soft to the touch. It's beautiful.

However, cotton is also a symbol of personal pain. The ends of the dried, woody base of the cotton boll can hurt and cut you if you don't pay attention when you handle it. I think it's an apt representation of my scalp since the inflammatory process associated with my form of alopecia — central centrifugal cicatricial alopecia (CCCA) — induces severe and disruptive pain.

This book is written for Black women experiencing CCCA, though, of course, other folks are welcome to read it, too. In it are lessons I've taken from experiencing hair loss, including larger insights about myself, and how I've come to recognize the terrible ways white supremacy has taken a toll on me.

If you are a Black woman experiencing hair loss — that includes cis women, transgender women, femmes, and nonbinary folk who relate to the experiences of Black women in this country — may this book serve you in realizing you are not alone in your questioning, emotions, and potentially the physical pain the hair loss process might bring. May it aid you in reflecting on your relationship to your hair and the experiences surrounding it, and may the insights and wisdom that surface serve your health and well-being in the highest and best ways.

If you are a Black woman with your hair intact, may this book aid you in reflecting on your relationship to your hair and the experiences surrounding it. And may it elevate your love, appreciation, and regard for your hair and the hair of the children in your life in the highest and best ways.

If you are a Black man, may this book help you understand the challenges of this journey, so you can be a non-judgmental and loving resource to the Black women in your life — especially those experiencing hair loss.

If you're not Black, may you come to understand just how deep and insidious racism and anti-Blackness are and cease further perpetuating it with misconceptions, judgments, and offenses. And may you stand against the discrimination of Black hair and Black bodies, and advo- cate for our right to wear our hair natural — however we choose, wherever we choose.

❖ ❖ ❖

I was diagnosed with CCCA at age 52. It's a form of scarring alopecia that almost exclusively affects Black women over the age of 30. Doctors can't definitively name the cause, though it's likely multifactorial, and there is no cure. The worst part for me — even more than losing my hair — is that I experience physical pain to a debilitating, tear-inducing, life-altering degree.

This journey has been difficult. I can't put it any other way. And I say this with full awareness that I'm one of the lucky women navigating it because I'm well-resourced. I have access to high-quality medical care, health insurance, and my very own personal care team: a loving husband, encouraging family and friends, understanding colleagues, and a host of professionals across multiple modalities that include conventional medicine, functional medicine, functional nutrition, mental health therapy, clinical herbalism, Ayurveda, acupuncture, and more. They've all guided and supported me along the way.

One of my care team members is an extraordinary therapist. She introduced me to writing exercises as a way of processing traumatic experiences and stopping the downward spiraling patterns of negative thought.

When I was distraught over the sudden loss of a dear friend, my therapist gave me an exercise: a six-word grief story. First, she had me write down a handful of words that described how I was feeling about my loss. Next, she asked me to write a short paragraph about each word. That exercise didn't ease the pain of losing my friend, but it did help me understand and face some heretofore unacknowledged feelings that were continuously present but subconsciously suppressed.

It seemed a good idea to apply this exercise to losing my hair — a different form of grief — so I began writing words in my journal that described my relationship to my hair from the time I was a young child until now, then I wrote words related to the stages I cycled through after being diagnosed with CCCA. I even discovered parallels between the cotton plant and its symbolism to American socioeconomics, the Black American experience, and Black hair. But writhing in pain while trying to keep up with work deadlines and obligations meant weeks passed before I settled on the right words.

The paragraphs took several months to complete, delayed by having to navigate a slow and burdensome medical system and spending hours on end poring over scientific literature to understand CCCA — all while wrestling with continued pain. The gift of this exercise was the full processing of my emotions and experiences, from which breakthroughs and revelations emerged. I wrote words and paragraphs about those too. By the time I finished this writing exercise, an entire year had passed and, to my surprise, I'd written a short book.

This is that book.

I occasionally shared what I learned from my writings with my care team — some who are Black and some who are not — and several of them encouraged me to publish what I'd written because my story is important. Because the stories of Black women are important. And because everyone needs to understand the experiences of Black women in this country in order for it to heal and recover from the past sins of its colonizing founding fathers.

My journey isn't over, but I stand in a place of strength. I've made peace with the possibility of total hair loss, and whether the process takes years or unfolds over decades, I will meet it with clarity, dignity, and unwavering self-compassion. For hair is not a source of my worth.

I AM THAT I AM.

"

Hair. It may seem like a mundane subject, but it has profound implications for how African American women experience the world.

- Lanita Jacobs–Huey[7]

[7] Jacobs-Huey, Lanita. *From the Kitchen to the Parlor: Language and Becoming in African American Women's Hair Care.* Oxford University Press, 2006.

PART 1

THE WEIGHT OF MY CROWN

ASSIMILATION

—————

" "

**The death of self-esteem can
occur quickly, easily in children,
before their ego has 'legs,' so to speak.**

- Toni Morrison, *The Bluest Eye*

PAIN

"Healing begins where the wound was made."

— Alice Walker, "The Way Forward Is with a Broken Heart"

BLOW DRYERS & HOT COMBS

My earliest memory of "wash day" goes back to when I was nine years old. I grew up in a three-bedroom 1,000 sq ft ranch-style house on the South Side of Chicago, where the kitchen and dining room flowed together as one continuous space. I remember lying on our tiny kitchen counter with my back on the hard surface, knees in the air, feet at my glutes, and head in the sink, while my mom washed, conditioned, comb-detangled, then loosely plaited my hair into four sections. The whole process took about 30 minutes, and it was painful. My back hurt. My neck hurt. And my scalp panged from the detangling, even though I kept still and my mom was caring and careful. She'd tightly squeeze the hair above where she was detangling to protect my scalp from feeling tugged, but she'd inevitably miss catching a few strands here and there as she worked in 2-inch sections of hair, conscientiously combing from ends to roots. When that happened, it felt as if my hair was being pulled right out of my scalp.

Next came blow drying. I'd sit in a chair at the dining table and my mom would stand over me, in her snap-button, round collar duster covered in pastel flowers, blow drying one section at a time. This was 1979, and I remember the teeth of the comb being super thin because blow dryer combs back then weren't made with tightly coiled hair in mind. If memory serves me right, it took about 30 minutes on the highest heat setting to take my 4 inches of shrunken, plaited hair to 8 inches because I was tender headed. Having that blow dryer comb pulled through my hair was painful, even though my mom was gentle. Sometimes the teeth would even break. Eventually, air concentrator nozzles were invented so you could hold a blow dryer in one hand and a detangling brush in the other, but that meant more intense heat and a different kind of pulling and tugging on my scalp.

After blow drying came the third comb: the pressing comb.

My mom kept a burner on the gas stove going for the entire 45 minutes it took to press my hair. Standing over me with my chair positioned next to the stove, Mom would set the metal comb in the flames — careful not to get the wooden handle too close to those flames — then apply bright blue hair grease to a section of my cotton-textured hair to protect it, while waiting for the comb to become hot enough to release a steady, wisp of smoke when she took it off the heat. If the comb was too hot, she'd cool it with four or five swift round-mouthed exhales, then run the hot pressing comb through the greased section of hair to straighten my tresses even more. I can still hear the soft crackle of the comb as it singed my strands, and I can recall the smell of my pressed hair — memorable not because the scent was pleasant, but because toasted, greased hair smells as amiss as a melting plastic doll. The whole time Mom was meticulous, therefore she'd cautiously get as close to my scalp as possible so my hair would lay as flat as possible. Occasionally, though, the comb would scrape my scalp, which burned like hell and occasionally left a sore.

Finally, styling my hair took another five to 45 minutes, depending on the 'do. My mom's simple and fast go-to look for me involved making a part down the middle of my head and plaiting two braids. For each side, she'd secure my hair at the base with a ponytail holder, then braid my hair and wrap the ends around the bar of a barrette to keep the braid intact and prevent my ends from fraying. If a special event like kindergarten graduation or Easter called for a fancier look, she'd use an electric curling iron to give me loose, "Shirley Temple" curls instead of braiding my hair. If she or I wanted to keep my curls going for a few days, Mom would apply tissue paper to the ends of my hair and roll it with pink, foam sponge rollers at night. My curls had a four-or-five-day lifespan before they'd stiffen and lose their hold, then Mom would resume plaiting my hair. On those mornings, she would often lay down my edges with a brush and occasionally some brown gel before swapping out my hair accessories to ensure the colors matched my school uniform or clothes.

Mom and I did our wash day routine about every two weeks for years. I was always jealous that my dad and brother got to relax during this time — my dad either reading the newspaper at the dining table or watching the news in the living room, and my brother watching a cartoon or sitcom in his bedroom.

Wash day was painful for me and difficult, if not painful, for my mom too. At the same time, it was a beautiful act of love on her part, and however our lives and emotions diverged later in life, I cherish these moments — for, as bell hooks wrote, "We learn about love in childhood."[8] When Mom finished my hair, we'd walk the short seven steps into my bedroom where we'd both look in the mirror. We'd smile at her finished product, then I would thank and hug her. She made me pretty, and I loved her for that and so much more.

---

[8] hooks, bell. *All about Love: New Visions.* 1st ed. William Morrow, 2000.

SALON SATURDAYS

At age 11 or 12, Mom decided I was old enough for a re-laxer, which meant I started having regular appointments with a professional hairdresser. Although she and I had grown accustomed to our bi-weekly ritual, shifting the re-sponsibility of my hair to someone else must have brought relief to my mom, despite it being an additional expense in a home where money was often tight.

My first relaxer was a "kiddie perm" — marketed as being gentler and, therefore, less effective than a regu-lar perm. I don't remember whether the kiddie perms hurt my scalp, but I do remember them not straightening my hair well or lasting very long. Mom would end up giving me curling iron touch-ups between hairstylist visits, especially my roots, which, like all Black girls with tightly coiled hair, routinely defied being tamed.

What I do remember is what happened when a hairdresser switched me to a regular perm in my early teens. We were at a large salon, at least by my neighbor-hood's standards, with each of four or five stylists working three to four clients at one time, and two assistants. The air was oppressive, with every person present incapable of escaping the stench of perm chemicals and the artificial fragrance of oil sheen. The stylist fulfilled her promise of a perfect perm because my hair got "beautifully straight," and I ended up with a scalp burn. Scalp burns happened because the regular perms we used back then (and may-be now, still) were made of lye, which burns when it's left too long on the scalp. Those burns turned into sores which took days to scab over and weeks to heal. It was no easy feat to comb my hair with sores on my scalp.

I got a "touch-up" every six to eight weeks, and I'd regularly get scalp burns in those initial years because I was too scared to speak up and tell the stylist my head was on fire. When I did speak up because the pain was unbearable, it often took stylists at least five to 10 more minutes to finish whatever they were doing with another client before they'd rinse out my perm. If my stylist had long fingernails or was "heavy-handed," shampooing my hair made the parts of my scalp that were burned hurt worse, and that torment was followed up with a blow dryer and curling iron.

I wouldn't stop relaxing my hair for 16 years, which means chemical relaxers have been applied to my head over one hundred times. My guess is that about fifteen of those applications resulted in scalp burns.

I endured this all in an effort to manipulate the magnificent, cotton-like texture of my hair into a more socially acceptable form: silk.

(SELF)LOATHING

"The master had said, 'You are ugly people.' They had looked about themselves and saw nothing to contradict the statement; saw, in fact, support for it leaning at them from every billboard, every movie, every glance. 'Yes,' they had said. 'You are right.' And they took the ugliness in their hands, threw it as a mantle over them, and went about the world with it."

— Toni Morrison, The Bluest Eye

For as long as I lived with my parents, I didn't have a choice about getting my hair straightened. It was expected because that's what my mom, dad, and the Black adults around me deemed a prerequisite for acceptance within and outside of our communities. Even when I reached 18 and was old enough to make the choice for myself, I, too, had thoroughly accepted that straight hair is "good hair." I came to believe that the straighter and more flowing my hair was, like those '90s shampoo commercials, the better I'd be regarded, even though a flowing state was only achievable for me within the first two or three days of getting my hair done.

Believing that natural Black hair — especially the tightly coiled, kinky type like mine — is "bad" hair is a mindfuck. I believed this for a long time because I'd been programmed by television, magazines, books, advertisements, family, and other people around me who verbalized their judgments about me or other Black girls and women. Two vivid examples come to mind:

The first occurred on a hot, mid-summer weekend in Chicago. It was the week after wash day, and with only window fans in the house to draw out the hot air, my hair did what was natural: it swelled and shrunk in concert with my sweat and the summertime humidity. I'd had my bedroom door closed all morning as a way of muffling the sounds in the kitchen and the TV in the living room that shared a wall with my bedroom. When I finally emerged from my room into the common area with my hair completely loose and looking like a collapsed 'fro, my dad, who was standing at the fridge, looked around at me, frowned, then said, "Your hair looks like a rat's nest."

I was eleven years old.

I adored my dad. He was fun, loving, always encouraging, and took great pride in my accomplishments. But his words were hurtful. They also marked a moment in time when I realized what would be required for a man to consider me attractive. My dad was very handsome and, because he was my father, his words and opinions mattered to me. His cruel words not only stung, but they became an amplification of the difference between us: my "rat's nest" and his wavy hair that wasn't necessarily "good" by racist standards, but considered "better" than mine. And he didn't have to work for his "better" hair. I can see him now, standing in the mirror of our bathroom in a white undershirt, black pants, and backless pleather slippers, taking a few seconds to pat a nickel-sized dab of pomade from an orange tin to his hair then making a dozen or so passes of his black, plastic comb through his hair to capture his signature wavy look. I assume he was oblivious to or unconcerned with the harsh tools and effort required to style my hair and the toll they took on me emotionally and physically. I wasn't allowed a break — not even in the comfort of my home.

Fast forward to age 14 when I was enrolled at an

all-girls', predominantly white, Catholic high school 10 miles away, where, if memory serves, there were only thirteen Black girls in my freshman class. Some of the white students were particularly inquisitive about Black hair, and two in particular singled out a few of us Black girls to ask how often we washed our hair. On a gorgeous, sunny day when we were spending time outdoors during a lunch break, they approached a Black classmate and me as we were walking from the parking lot toward the back entrance of the school. When these two white girls asked us their question, my classmate responded with genuine honesty: "Every two weeks." Fearing it was a trap, I lied and said, "Every week," as if that would be an acceptable response.

They gave us a snide look and as they walked away, I heard one say to the other, "That is so gross."

I was both shocked and hurt. They made me feel small and ashamed of a perfectly appropriate wash regimen for my hair texture. Thank goodness for the one Black teacher at my high school, Ms. S, who would periodically hold space for the Black students to talk through our experiences. That day, among the six or so of us huddled together in her homeroom — sitting and standing outside the line of sight from the front and back doors — I shared what happened earlier and she helped me process it.

Ms. S was always kind to us, and I enjoyed being in her presence and hearing her speak in her sweet, singsong voice. She was also beautiful and sharply dressed, with skin the color of creamed coffee and a perfectly cut bob. I never could figure out whether her hair was permed or natural; I just knew it was perfect every time I saw her.

When Ms. S had something important to say, her voice took on a monotone quality, except for the words she chose to emphasize by speaking them at a much louder volume. I can't recall all that she said, but I do remember that she spoke with a great deal of emphasis that day. Her bottom line message to us was this: What those girls thought about our hair meant nothing because we are children of God and therefore perfect exactly as we are.

Ms. S helped me heal the wound but, even today, I still have the scar.

These experiences, among others, played a crucial role in shaping my understanding of how both Black and white people perceived my hair. They influenced my feelings about it and, importantly, determined the extreme lengths I'd go to straighten it so I could conform to white beauty standards. My feelings of self-consciousness and embarrassment about my hair's natural state was a form of self-loathing. I wouldn't have called it that then, however, I most certainly recognize and can name it as such now.

And my self-loathing went deep. Deep enough that I developed an unhealthy fascination with Black boys with wavy hair, as a means of becoming "good hair" proximate. I'm not proud to admit it now; still, it's my unfortunate truth.

Much like Pecola Breedlove wishing for blue eyes in Toni Morrison's novel *The Bluest Eye*, myriad times in my childhood I wished for hair like Lonette McKee in Sparkle, with its soft texture, dark color, and long flawless curls. There was a time when I would have considered it a blessing, like Pecola, if I crossed the threshold into madness, because then I might be beautiful to others and, therefore, to myself.

OBSESSION

"Hair is hair — yet also about larger questions: self-acceptance, insecurity and what the world tells you is beautiful."

— Chimamanda Ngozi Adichie[9]

At 18, I landed my first job through a summer internship program that placed me with one of the Big Six accounting firms. All the people I worked with every summer for four years were white, as well as the vast majority of the people I came into contact with during the workday. I felt out of place being the "the only one." Being younger than everyone else and not having common interests or shared experiences around most things, including food, music, dating, and marriage, made me feel even more like an outsider.

Hyper-aware of my appearance, I minimized how much I stood out by buying clothes that looked like what everyone else wore (navy, black and white, gray, beige, and sometimes red in color), eating the food they ate for lunch (salads with unfamiliar ingredients, sandwiches with tahini, pesto, and other strange sauces), and wearing my hair as close as I could to how they wore theirs ("bone straight"). If my roots weren't lying flat in the morning, I'd tame them with a curling iron before leaving for work. And every day at work, I'd visit the bathroom several times — especially after coming back from lunch — to ensure my hair was falling just right. If rain, humidity, or sweat caused my hair to shrink and swell on the way to work, I felt embarrassed the whole day.

---

[9] Kellaway, Kate. "Chimamanda Ngozi Adichie: 'My New Novel Is about Love, Race... and Hair.'" Books. *The Guardian*, April 6, 2013. https://www.theguardian.com/theobserver/2013/apr/07/chimamanda-ngozi-adichie-americanah-interview.

This obsession with not wanting a hair on my head out of place lasted a decade. And it didn't matter that my boyfriend at the time — who became my husband three years later — always found this bemusing because short, natural hair was the look he most loved on Black women. I bought into the lies of the dominant culture, which adversely impacted my mind and body. It would also cost me a great deal in terms of time and money.

Just like cotton was harvested in the name of wealth building for colonizers at the cost of Black bodies, the American beauty industry is disproportionately funded by Black consumers at the cost of our health.

EXPENSE

"We're serious about our hair. It shows up in how we spend our money and how we spend our time."

— Cheryl Grace, SVP Community Alliance and Community Engagement, Nielsen[10]

TIME

Visits to the hairdresser every two weeks meant spending a minimum of three hours in the salon — maybe five hours if my mom and I had appointments on the same day — because, again, our stylists were usually working multiple clients at once. The same was true throughout my experiences at salons during my college days in Chicago and during my early years of full-time employment in Washington, D.C.

I remember reading an article in the AFRO American Newspaper that said 18 percent of Black women spend more than three hours at hair salon appointments — triple the average of all women surveyed: 6 percent.[11]

By the time I was in my mid-twenties, I was frequenting one of the top salons in my Maryland neighborhood outside of D.C., first every other week, then weekly. My stylist was supremely talented and in high demand, hence her schedule was packed with a client coming in the door every fifteen minutes. Consequently, I was routinely in her salon for long hours, and around holidays — when every waiting area chair, wash bowl, dryer seat, and stylist chair was occupied, and women sat cramped together on a

---

[10] *The High Costs of Black Women's Hair*. The Glam Gap. BET, 2019. 901. https://www.bet.com/video-clips/1bo8ch/the-glam-gap-the-high-costs-of-black-women-s-hair.

[11] Special to the AFRO. "The Afro Tax: African American Women Spend Four Times More on Hair Care than Caucasian Women." AFRO American Newspapers, April 12, 2023. http://afro.com/the-afro-tax-african-american-women-spend-four-times-more-on-hair-care-than-caucasian-women/.

bench queued up for a wash bowl, out of focus within the unyielding fog of oil sheen — it might be six or seven hours.

Given how fixated I was with my hair, it's no surprise that I jumped at the chance of a standing appointment when my stylist announced openings for Tuesday mornings. I didn't even blink at the five o'clock start time.

Getting up at 4:00 a.m. every week for a 5:00 a.m. hair appointment was impractical. Nevertheless, I did this routine every week for years because I needed that frequency to keep my hair not just straight, but as flowing as possible.

COST

"We roughly spend three times more the dollars than [a] Caucasian woman. So even though we only make up 8% of the population, we are spending roughly 25% of the dollars in the U.S. haircare market."

— Erica "Sister Scientist" Douglas[12]

In the 1990s, my salon visits averaged $450 a month for a combination of regular visits, touch-ups, cuts, and color. I looked up what a few top salons in that area charge now, and I estimate that I'd spend about $750 to $1,000 a month in today's dollars for those same services. Some of these costs — wash, blow dry, cut, color — are spent by all women on their haircare routines, regardless of ethnicity. But let there be no mistake, Black women with tight coils pay an extra hair tax in the form of relaxers, weaves, wigs, and frequency of salon visits to wear silky, shiny, straight hair.

The tighter your coils, the higher your "tax." There is injustice in hair care too.

---

[12] *The High Costs of Black Women's Hair*. The Glam Gap. BET.

LIMITATION

**"Straightened hair has always seemed to me to call
attention to the desire for hair to stay in place."**

— bell hooks, "Straightening Our Hair"

Keeping my hair bone straight meant I couldn't sweat or expose my hair to wind, humidity, or rain. That eliminated regular exercise, driving with the car windows down, and spending long periods of time outdoors. Maintaining straight hair was such a limiting factor that it impacted not just my mental health and sense of self-worth, but my time, bank account, and physical health because of low vitamin D levels and weight gain that was unhealthy for me.

Around age 27, I made a wonderful new friend from Puerto Rico who introduced me to salsa music. There is something about the ornate rhythm of congas, the sharp accents of the clave, the joyful blare of brass instruments, the gorgeous piano melodies, and simple lyrics made beautiful by being sung in Spanish that makes you feel exuberant and compels you to dance. Though sweat was the enemy of my relaxed hair, I loved salsa dancing! My friend and I became part of a lovely community of people with whom I went dancing almost every weekend, and it took just a couple of months for me to become fed up with straightening my hair. It helped that by that point I'd begun questioning the whole notion of "good hair."

So, at age 28, I made the decision to go natural.

RESISTANCE

---

66 99

**Freeing yourself was one thing.
Claiming ownership of that
freed self was another.**

- Toni Morrison, *Beloved*

LEAP

TWA

I shared my decision with my stylist (who'd been doing my hair for several years at that point) and she was encouraging. We agreed that at the next appointment, she'd do the "big chop," and I'd get a texturizer on my teeny-weeny afro (TWA) to make it softer and a wee bit curly. (I realize now that this was an "I'm going natural, *but*..." moment). Although I wasn't aware of it at the time, I think I was hoping for hair like my dad's: not "good," but "better." Even in this bold step, I was clinging to white supremacist programming.

As it turned out, a texturizer did nothing for me; my hair still required a ton of product to create defined curls. The product my stylist used was marketed as a frizz-control serum and I'm pretty sure I used a whole palm-size amount on my TWA after each wash. In return, it permanently stained all my pillows (even the dark colored ones), dried out and dulled my hair, and after going dancing one night with it dripping down my neck — nearly causing my dance partner to drop me during a neck dip — I realized I couldn't continue this faux natural game anymore.

Something more had to give.

LOC EXTENSIONS

I'd been thinking about loc'ing my hair since before my "big chop" and I knew I'd get there eventually. By this time, it was the late 1990s and I was seeing more Black women wear their hair natural — maybe two out of 10 Black women on the subway every day, compared to the two women I used to see in an entire week.

A stylist at my salon wore locs the entire time I frequented that business and I always thought her hair was beautiful. She was somewhat tall and brown-skinned like me, and her locs went a third of the way down her back. I thought wearing locs would be a lot of fun (and much easier) than battling a growing 'fro. The sticky point was I didn't have patience for the awkward stage where it takes a year or more for the locs to form, plus I assumed "messy" locs would be more risky to my professional career than my untapered 'fro.

My stylist, who always kept pace with every trend and regularly exposed herself to new techniques, got trained in loc extensions. When I saw her with her own shoulder-length set, I fully committed. Loc extensions were the perfect solution to the awkward starting-out stage, plus I could have long locs right from the start, as my stylist had, which would be easy to gather in a low bun to keep them neat and out of reach.

Loc extensions cost $2,000 at that time — very expensive, yet understandable because each loc was hand-made with human hair and required a couple of days to install using needle and thread. It took over a year for me to save that much money. By the time I did, it was 2001 and I was working for a nonprofit where I could "get away" with wearing locs instead of a corporate accounting firm with a dress code that repudiated natural Black hair. While I don't recall whether the corporate dress code specifically forbade afros and other Black hairstyles, there was certainly an implicit dress code that left little doubt. I remember the day I walked into the office with my TWA: a white male partner at the firm looked at me, and said to my face that my haircut was "radical."

FREEDOM

I'd not long been 31 when my loc extension appointment arrived. I was the only person in the salon other than my stylist on that Monday, yet I could distinguish the slight smell of hair products lingering in the air — oil spray, relaxers, shampoo that smelled like candy, and pomade. (Or maybe it was all in my mind, having been conditioned by prior visits). It took eight hours for my stylist to install half the locs and I returned the following Monday for her to finish. Sitting in a chair for that long, with only a short lunch break and a couple of bathroom breaks made my whole body stiff and achy. But it was worth it.

When I walked out of the salon with a head full of locs on a crisp, winter evening in January, I felt ecstatic! And more than that, I felt free. Free from the burden of ever having to get another silk press, and free from fussing over my hairstyles because locs require no tool or treatment to be fabulous. It was the most liberating moment of my entire life — more than leaving my parents' home to begin living on my own. And my husband was positively happy for me.

For the entire time I wore locs, I never *needed* to wake up and "style" my hair unless I wanted to. I never had to run a comb, brush, blow dryer, or curling iron through my hair. And the weather on a given day was inconsequential. Rain? Bring it. My hair loved the moisture. Snow? Bring that too — more moisture! Wind? Didn't impact my hair one bit. Humidity? Well, that's just another form of moisture (although it would make me sweat out my roots). My loc'd hair thrived in all weather. For the first time in my life, I could be outdoors anytime, all the time. I was free.

Beautifully and unapologetically free.

MISSED EXPECTATIONS

UNIFORMITY

Being loc'd should have been all sunshine and roses. It wasn't because I had expectations that my locs would be perfect. They weren't.

For starters, I discovered my loc extensions weren't permanent. The first time I went dancing with my shoulder-length locs, allowing them to swing with every turn — an experience that added to the joy and fun of dancing — I got home and realized an extension had fallen out. This ended up happening to about a fifth of the extensions in my head. It seemed like every other visit required that my stylist sew an extension or two back in. She never charged me for that, and she made sure they didn't fall out a second time by reinforcing the thread. The tradeoff, unfortunately, was the clearly visible thread on the outside of those locs, which made me self-conscious. Additionally, the sizes of my locs, as they grew out, were different from the sizes of many of the extensions, and that differentiation was noticeable. This made me even more self-conscious.

My self-consciousness only deepened after I realized my stylist didn't do the best job with the size and spacing of each loc section. Instead of making evenly spaced,

Excursus

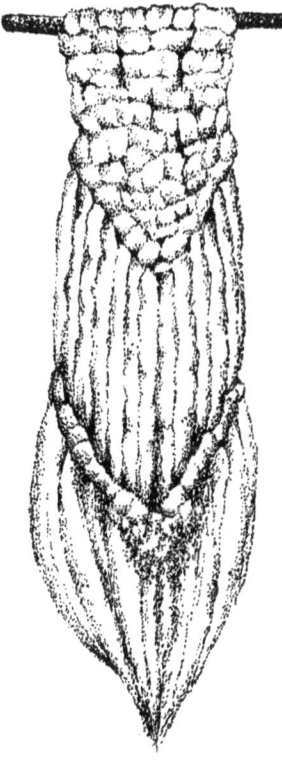

Styling locs is like crafting macramé. A few years ago, I took a macramé class at an interior design studio for fun and weaved this beautiful pattern with cotton yarn. My macramé was unique; it was unlike every other person's in the class, even from those who chose the same pattern.

As I looked at this macramé on the door of my office while writing this excursus, I realized just how much locs are like thick, cotton yarn. Both are sturdy in that they hold their form and stay in place as you weave segments together to create intricate patterns of knots and loops. And both are fragile, as strands of cotton or hair gather around your fingers when you pull at the ends to create a tapered shape.

Woven loc styles are beautiful works of art like macramé. And they are a testament to Black heritage and individuality.

diamond shaped parts all over my scalp, I suspected she parted each section according to the size loc she made, and those sizes varied. That meant my actual locs would never be uniform, nor would my locs ever fall in perfect alignment... unless I started over, which was never gonna happen.

UPDOS

It took four years for my natural locs to reach shoulder length — which was important to me because I wanted the option to wear a low bun — and only then did I give my stylist the okay to cut the extensions. That chop was most satisfying because, finally, my locs were 100% my own and each loc was, at least, individually uniform. Shortly after this cut, I transitioned to a natural hair specialist in Maryland, a bit closer to D.C.

My new stylist was an expert in locs and endlessly creative, so I looked forward to wearing a multitude of updos. This is one of the beautiful things about locs: you can sculpt them into an infinite number of styles that can last for weeks. Sculptability is a beautiful feature of Black hair generally, and locs take that to a whole new level.

I felt heartbroken when I discovered I couldn't sustain any tension on my scalp, though perhaps I should have known this, given how tender headed I was as a child. The tension from a tight updo always gave me a headache that wouldn't go away until I took the updo down. The only style I could consistently manage myself was a technique taught to me by my husband's colleague.

One day, when I accompanied him to his office, I met the department's executive assistant — a gorgeous, ebony-skinned, middle-aged woman with long locs that were collected into the most intricate bun atop her head. I complimented her on her hairstyle and she graciously offered to show me how to create it. She gathered a handful of my locs at the crown of my head into a small bun, took two locs at a time and wrapped them around the bun before tucking the ends at the base of the bun — the bun growing larger with each wrap in alternating directions. I was sold! And the best part about this cute new look was I could achieve it with minimal effort and zero tension.

Wearing my locs loose, in two-strand twists, or this one updo was beautiful and I loved it, but I felt cheated because there was this whole other experience that other Black women and men were having that I couldn't. I was free, but not as happy as I expected I'd be, or that I thought I should be.

OBSESSION 2.0

In the same way I'd been obsessed with keeping my relaxed hair straight, I was obsessed with keeping my roots looking like they were freshly twisted. But my roots never liked being tamed in my relaxer years, therefore I should have known they'd resist being tamed in my loc'd years.

Early on in my loc'd years, I experimented with no less than 10 different styling gels hoping one of them would hold the twist at my roots. Because I didn't know about interlocking techniques at that time, I'd retwist my locs then use a clip to keep them down until the gel dried about three mornings each week. In spite of my efforts to hold onto a "fresh maintenance" look, it would take less than an hour of moving about before the twists would un-ravel. If I danced — especially flamenco, my new passion — 1.5 to two inches of untamed roots would be on full display.

None of this deterred me. It just meant I had to retwist all 120 of my locs tightly before class and secure them with hair ties, then keep them bundled up for a couple of hours until my roots dried. When I learned how to inter-lock, it made things easier, but I remained obsessed with the 16 or so locs along my front edge and the locs at the very top of my head. Most mornings, I'd still gel and retwist them.

As I reflect on that time, I realize that my obses-sion with my locs masked a deeper insecurity: because Black women are stigmatized for wearing our hair natural, I didn't want people to look at me and think my hair was unkempt. It's funny to me now that, even though I made a clear deci-sion to resist the beauty standards of the dominant culture, I was still allowing myself to be held hostage by them.

So much for embracing my newfound freedom.

HOSTILITY

BLACK PEOPLE

When my father first saw me with locs he said to me, for the second and final time in my life, and with more disgust than the first, that my hair looked like a "rat's nest." My mother was never hostile toward me about it, but she re-directed her negative feelings to my brother, to whom she had lots to say about my hair. My grandmother was passive aggressive. The first time she saw me with locs she shook her head. A short while later, when looking through old photos of me with my hair relaxed, she said, "That was my favorite hairstyle on you." Of course, each of them loved me as much as they always did; they just didn't care for my hair and they made their feelings clear.

There were countless experiences I had of being in a room with strangers — Black men and straight-haired Black women — who'd look my way, smirk, then whisper about me to each other. I don't recall any of them ever saying something to me directly about my hair, but they didn't have to. It was obvious whenever my presence served as fodder for their entertainment. Black people can love each other fiercely; we can also denigrate one another in equal measure.

It took years for me to reach a place where I no longer cared what anyone thought about my hair because I had done the internal work of freeing myself from being tied to anything but my own beauty standards. To presume locs are disgusting or not as attractive as straightened hair is bigoted. And while Black people don't wield the broad institutional power white people do, I believe Black people can uphold and reinforce white supremacist views.

This makes me reflect on the role of Black overseers and other enslaved people on the plantation. There were times when there wasn't a white face as far as the eye could see, but Black people in the cotton fields knew they remained at risk of violence if everyone didn't meet the enslaver's expectations. My family and the Black people who'd sneer at me weren't going to scold or beat me for wearing my hair loc'd. They certainly weren't overseers and they likely didn't even consciously care about upholding white supremacist beauty standards. But I recognized their fear over my non-conformance. Fear born of a desire for personal safety because 'acceptability' is a safeguard. I can't blame them for wanting safety for themselves and for me, but I can say this: Sometimes we still do the work of oppression for white people, and that's just one of many legacies of white supremacy across the globe.

WHITE PEOPLE

A white flamenco teacher of mine, when she first saw me with locs, said she couldn't understand why Black women would "ruin" their hair by getting "braids." (She was far from the only white person to mistakenly call my locs braids). As we stood together near the mirrors at the front of the studio, for about 30 seconds she proceeded to tell me how braids made Black women's hair fall out. I was stunned silent and couldn't muster a response before she walked away. That's what happens to me in high stress situations: I freeze. I never did say anything to her. Fifty-two-year-old me would have choice words for her, but thirty-one-year-old me hadn't yet developed a strong voice.

One day, while traveling on a plane for work, the gorgeous and friendly flight attendant working my section of the plane saw me and announced out loud that she was looking forward to her newly-loc'd hair getting as long as mine, which by then reached half-way down my back. I was in the middle seat between a white woman and white man, and the white woman in the aisle seat turned towards me after the flight attendant's compliment, and asked, "Can I touch it?" Without looking me in the eye or waiting for a response, she grabbed a hold of one of my locs, twirled it between her thumb and forefinger, and said, "Wow. It doesn't even feel like hair." After she let my hair go, she turned back toward her daughter who was sitting in the opposite aisle seat and resumed the conversation they'd been having. She never once looked me in the eye.

What the fuck?

That is a microaggression — no, it's an aggression *and* a microassault. In keeping with my natural response to stress, I froze and never said anything, though I was traumatized and I wanted to tell that flight attendant she should know better than to make a comment about Black hair in front of white people (especially white women) because they often seize it as an opportunity to ambush Black women with infelicitous questions and violate our personhood with inappropriate and unwelcome touch.

There would be other times white people would touch my hair without my permission.

The incident that most stands out in my mind occurred during a business dinner at a hip restaurant in D.C. with three colleagues — one woman and two men. The restaurant was large and bustling with most seats occupied, yet the acoustics allowed for unstrained table conversation and eavesdropping on the tables to my left and right when laughter piqued my curiosity. At some point in the conversation with my colleagues, each one stood up from their seats and walked behind me to run their hands through my locs. I don't recall what was said about my hair prior to this happening, but I was stunned silent again! And I was very aware of the Black couple seated at the table to my left, in particular, who saw what transpired and looked just as stunned as I. I stopped eavesdropping after that because I didn't want to know what they may have said about what happened to me, and I couldn't move or say anything for a whole interminable minute. I wanted to scream and curse at my colleagues, but I kept running "Black math" calculations in my mind: If I go off, will this affect my job? Would the incident be relayed to other colleagues and the finger pointed at me for causing a scene? Would the restaurant manager ask me to leave? Would the police be called? Would they force me to apologize?

I knew I couldn't just let it go and, even though my voice still hadn't gotten strong, after I regained my composure, I settled on sarcasm as the safest response and said, loud enough for both tables next to me to hear, "I feel like I'm in a petting zoo."

I intended my sarcasm to make a point, but those white people were so clueless they thought my words were hilarious and laughed out loud. I've often wished my response to stressful situations was to fight because I might have slapped all three, same for that woman on the plane, my dance teacher, and every other white person who has said something obnoxious about my hair or put their hands on my locs without my consent.

But had I done that, we know this Black woman would've been the one in jail.

I don't believe most white people would go up to a stranger, a colleague, or even a friend who is white and put their hands in that white person's hair. Yet, white people feel entitled to do that to Black people, which tells me exactly what they think of me and their position in relation to me. I used the term "petting zoo" with my colleagues for a reason: it suggests that, deep down, they see me as a curiosity, less a person and more like an animal, or, at the very least, they see me as undeserving of the same level of respect they'd show another white person. This is how racism works. And any white person claiming it's just curiosity, admiration, or anything else but racism when they choose to violate my bodily sovereignty is lying to themself.

OTHER PEOPLE OF COLOR

Anti-Blackness is worldwide, therefore it's not a shock to me that other people of color would be hostile towards me because of my natural hair.

When I was passing through the gates of the busy airport in Lima, Peru, to catch a flight back to the U.S. after hiking the Inca Trail, the two Latina gate attendants checking boarding passes looked at me snidely as I approached, then at each other, and laughed. While they didn't say anything directly to me, I knew the focus of the exchange was my hair since my bald, racially-ambiguous looking husband, nor the dozens of white and Latina people in front of us, got that response when they walked through the gates before me.

Some of you readers may see these words and think, fairly, that this might not have had anything to do with my hair. But when you've experienced as many of those looks as I have, you just *know*. Could it have been insecurity or a projection on my part? Possibly. But I doubt it. My mind knows anti-Blackness when I see it, and more than that, my body knows it when I experience it.

APPRECIATION

Luckily, every act of hostility or racism I've faced has been met with respect, appreciation, or admiration.

A Black woman would approach me on the street or in a place of business and tell me how much they liked or loved my locs at least once a month. Some even told me how much they admired my bravery, which always felt bittersweet. I wore my hair loc'd for 20 years, so that's at least 240 times Black women have shown me and my locs love.

Black men showed me love too — often through passing comments on the street. Most felt genuine and free of misogynoir, a term coined by Black feminist scholar Moya Bailey in 2008 to describe the specific blend of racism and misogyny directed at Black women. Still, there were moments when a compliment came at the expense of other Black women. I remember, not too long after getting my loc extensions, a Black man approached me on the subway in D.C. and said, "Thank you for wearing your hair natural in the 'weave capital of the world.'" Yikes. It's uncomfortable and unsettling to receive a compliment tinged with disrespect or contempt for other Black women.

White women were even complimentary, especially starting in the 2010s. For example, every time I visited my dentist's office, when the hygienist asked the doctor to perform her post-cleaning check-up, the doctor said to me, "I like your hair." She's been saying that to me for several years, no matter my hairstyle. I admit, I sometimes questioned whether the compliments were sincere or if they were placating guilt about things white women once thought or said about Black women and our hair. I could never be sure.

Earnest respect, appreciation, and admiration was always pleasing, still nothing felt better than the respect, appreciation, and admiration I showed myself — achieved only after years of self-reflection. I embraced my natural hair, was proud of being natural, and felt fortunate and grateful for reaching a point and place in my professional career where wearing my hair natural couldn't limit me or be used against me in any consequential way.

NEXT-LEVEL AUTHENTICITY

I started coloring my hair in my mid-20s for the sheer fun of it. I liked having a burgundy tint to my hair one day and a copper tint another. On bright, sunny days, my hair was the hit!

When gray strands started to come through in my late 20s, what was once an option to color my hair became pressure. By the time I counted 20 gray strands at the top of my head, I began coloring my hair every six weeks. And when I reached my mid-40s, I started getting my roots dyed every three weeks. I'd returned to using chemicals consistently, this time to hide a different aspect of myself: my age. By this time I was living in Baltimore, which meant traveling 1.5 to 2 hours to see my stylist during the workday — a 5-hour commitment when all was said and done.

There is such pressure for women to hide our age. We feel that pressure in multiple ways, and one is because we're seen as less attractive as we grow older. I've seen count-less men with younger women, but I can count on one hand the number of times I've seen older women with younger men. It almost always goes one way. Men can age, but wom-en must look as young as possible for as long as possible.

Clearly, I was no more immune to gender-based programming than I was to race-based programming. But just like with my relaxed hair, I reached a point where enough was enough.

When I turned 47, I made the decision to no longer dye my hair to hide the gray. I was aiming for 100-percent natural hair by the time I was 50 and, though I knew it would be an awkward few years, I was committed. And I never wavered.

BOLDNESS

I saw the first Black Panther film twice, back-to-back, when it was released in 2018. At the wise age of 48, I appreciated it for the beautiful and extraordinary celebration of Blackness that it was. To this day, if there was a genie who could grant me three wishes, one of my wishes would be to live in Wakanda.

The characters I most admired were the Dora Milaje warriors. They were strong, fierce, powerful, and magnificently beautiful with their shaved heads. I wasn't courageous enough to go full-on Dora Milaje and shave my whole head, but I was inspired to shave the sides and the back of my head. It gave me an edginess I liked.

I became bold in my own way though. Not just with how I wore my hair, but how I showed up in the world. Wearing my hair natural helped me grow and evolve as a human. It helped me love and accept people as they are. It infused me with courage. And that courage helped me cultivate the ability to name what I witness and to speak out against racism, sexism, homophobia, transphobia, non-binary hatred, and other forms of oppression. I finally found my voice. Something I'd been striving for my whole life.

Excursus

Racism is used to justify all manner of sins personal (stereotyping, stigmatizing, racial profiling, violence, bullying, harassment, microaggressions, microassaults) and transpersonal (slavery, Jim Crow, redlining, employment discrimination, the denial of reparations, the use of race-based equations to estimate biological function, mass incarceration). Race is a fiction with no biological basis, yet it has been used to position white people at the top of our national caste and Black people at the bottom. It is by design that we are seen as less worthy of power, resources, and respect.

Black people in the U.S. are as resilient as the cotton our ancestors picked, and we're weary. We're hastily aging. We're physically ill. We're dying early. A lifetime of "weathering"[13] the insidious, cumulative effects of racism and racial injustice will do this. And fuck the personal-responsibility narrative, as if our health issues could be solved if each of us would just make "better" choices.

Despite Black people's continued absorption of racism's effects into every cell of our bodies — much like cotton absorbs liquid into every fiber — we endure. We withstand the injustices like the cotton plant withstands harsh winds, pounding rain, and scorching heat. And we do our best to resist erosion like cotton resists the boll weevils who feed on it. Still, these conditions exact their toll.

I may be weary and prematurely gray, with an increased number of health issues, but I'm here. And I'm grateful to be a line leader for my ancestors who guide me, power my steps, and motivate me to rise and thrive regardless of the weather.

[13] "Weathering" is a term first coined by public health researcher Dr. Arline T. Geronimus in her 1992 article titled, "The weathering hypothesis and the health of African-American women and infants: evidence and speculations."

DISSATISFACTION

LOC EXTENSIONS, ROUND 2

In documenting my relationship to my hair, I realized that for every two steps forward, I'd take a step back.

Having the sides and back of my head shaved was wonderful, *and* I had the expectation that I'd still be able to wear my hair down. However, my locs never fell the way they should have because the loc sections weren't installed evenly, and now that nonuniformity was very pronounced. Consequently, I'd only wear it up.

Since I couldn't handle any tension on my scalp, my stylist had a fun way of creating a loose fishtail braid from back to front and then pinning it on the side. I never knew about this technique before and I liked it. However, where my hair was shaved in the back was right where the thickest and most uneven loc sections were, so when I got a fresh maintenance you could really notice the imperfections. That bothered me, which is why most of the time I reverted to the updo technique I learned from my husband's colleague. It got old quick.

Two years later, I decided I'd return to a full head of locs. I knew the technique for installing loc extensions had come a long way and involved a crochet hook vs. needle and thread, so I bought pre-made locs online and found a stylist who specialized in loc extensions to put them in. The pre-made locs ended up being larger than I hoped, and the process of installing them was painful, but at least I didn't feel as self-conscious, and the gray loc extensions covered up some of the still part-gray,-part-copper locs when I wore my updo.

To my great disappointment, the loc extensions didn't take because my hair, which softens and flattens when wet — just like cotton — wouldn't hold the extensions. With each wash, between two to seven would fall out. To find myself in this place with extensions for the second time was upsetting. The stylist who put them in did her best to reinstall the ones that fell out, but after a few cycles of this, enough was enough for her and she suggested I cut off my locs and wear a TWA because I'd be "cute as a button." She even turned me onto some educational resources to learn about products and techniques I could use to bring out my natural curl pattern. I read the websites she gave me plus dozens more, and I watched just as many videos to learn how to style a TWA to get myself comfortable with taking that leap again.

TWA, ROUND 2

By this point, I was 51, and life was highly stressful for a few reasons. My work as a full-time consultant was intense, overwhelming, and difficult. I had a hysterectomy in September due to fibroids, which placed extreme stress on my physical body. And I was dissatisfied and stressed about my hair. Again.

Major surgery has a way of putting things into perspective. While I intuited I'd come through surgery just fine, there was always a possibility the surgery could go wrong, and that made me reflect on my life and state of happiness. Were my close relationships mutually supportive and nurturing? Was I living up to my full potential at work? Did I do right by people familiar and unknown? Was the world a little better because I was here? Was I generally happy?

In my reflections I realized just how much I was grateful for. I was loved. My closest relationships were deeply fulfilling. I felt safe and secure at home. I was doing impactful work with mission-based organizations committed to a better and more just world. And I had no regrets.

Still, three things needed to shift to make life more joyful. First, I had to let go of the belief that hard work alone defined my worth. Second, I needed to focus only on work that I felt most passionate about. And third, it was time to release the negative thought patterns I held around my hair — the most central expression of my Blackness — once and for all.

A few weeks after my surgery at my next hair appointment, I had my regular stylist cut off all my locs.

It was a drastic change, and one that felt even more liberating than locs, especially because I was finally all salt-and-pepper. 100-percent natural! My husband adored my new look. In fact, it was his favorite hairstyle of any I'd worn before, and he thought my gray was gorgeous. But that whole idea of "wash and go" styling to "bring out one's natural curl pattern" didn't work for me.

In every YouTube video I watched, all the women ended up with thick, shiny curls. But my kinky hair, full of disobedient strands of gray, wouldn't look like that no matter what products I applied or how much of them I used. I will also admit, now, after more reflection, that my quest to bring out my natural curl pattern was yet another attempt at having hair that looked like my dad's. After 20 years of wearing locs, I found myself, yet another time, unconsciously reaching toward white adjacency.

Eventually, I checked myself and bought a black sponge with 1/4" holes and a tiny tennis racket-like device because I was intent on letting go of products and getting some added texture in an easier, simpler, and cheaper way. I wanted additional texture because when my TWA was picked out, the combination of a rounded shape and a lot of gray made me feel like I was 70 or 80, and I wasn't ready to look that old. I loved picked-out TWAs on the elderly Black women in my life; I just didn't love the same look on me — not yet. This was internalized ageism at work.

Well, it turns out neither of those tools worked on my hair. No matter what I did, I couldn't get those cute sponge or tennis-racket curls to form. My stylist even gave it a shot, then shrugged, "Nope. Not happening."

SATISFACTION

At a subsequent visit, my stylist suggested finger coils for a textured look and I was thrilled with the finished product. They look like fresh starter locs and, when I slept on them, they flattened out such that when I woke up I looked a little bit like I had small sponge curls after all. It took manual work to get them, which was challenging for me to do in the back of my head where I couldn't see. Even so, they were fun, age-appropriate to me, and I loved them.

For the first time in my life, I was completely satisfied with my hair. I had a style that looked good and with which I couldn't find fault.

Oh, but why did this deep-in-my-bones satisfaction have to be short-lived?

Like grief, the stages of hair loss aren't linear.

Most days, I cycle through more than one.

PART II

THE LOSS THAT UNRAVELED ME

Content Note: This section includes references to suicidal thoughts and mental health struggles. Reader discretion is advised. If you or someone you know is struggling, resources are listed at the end of this book.

DENIAL

———

In January, three and a half months after getting TWA #2, I noticed two half-inch bald spots at the front of my head. My reaction mirrored the first time I saw a mouse dropping on my kitchen counter: I chose to ignore it because I couldn't handle the reality of what it meant: Where there's one, there's more. Plus, with my cotton-like hair texture, I could easily conceal those bald spots.

In March, my stylist noticed those same spots and more along the edges of and within the crown of my head. She suggested I see a dermatologist, so I made an appointment for June — the earliest I could get.

In the meantime, I began to experience pain after washing my hair every seven to 10 days. At the time I wondered if I'd developed an allergy to ingredients in one of my hair products, however, I chose to ignore that too. After all, my stylist and I had been using those same products for fifteen years and, if they hadn't bothered me before, it didn't seem likely they would bother me now.

My first dermatologist, a Black man, came to my attention years before when someone mentioned him at my hair salon. A fellow client talked about a special lotion he created for a woman experiencing hair loss. At the time, hair loss didn't seem relevant to me; I was simply glad to have the name of a Black dermatologist in that area whom I could reach out to if needed. Little did I know, it would become pertinent to my life later on.

When I arrived at his office, located in an old, 10-story office building, I felt anxious. It took me an hour to get there from Baltimore, and I waited close to an hour to be seen. There were several things I took note of while I waited. The aloof disposition of the receptionist. The television showing ads for dermatological services, on repeat. The carpet, white walls, and the dingy fake wood paneling, that appeared as if no one had touched them in decades. The sign on the wall that read "No Cell Phones" and the other one thanking me for my patience. The condescending way the doctor was speaking to a couple in one of the three treatment rooms down the hall.

The dermatologist was about 6'3" and in his early 70s. After escorting me back to one of his four treatment rooms, he asked me to share what was going on. My telling of the story must not have been fast enough or to his satisfaction, because he interrupted me no less than ten times with pointed questions that didn't allow for a full relaying of everything I was experiencing.

After five minutes of discussing my hair, he took another minute to examine my scalp with gloved hands, then diagnosed me with having alopecia areata, which he said would either stop and reverse itself or worsen and extend to all the hair on my body. His delivery was just like that — matter-of-fact and not at all sensitive. He wrote a prescription for clobetasol, a topical steroid lotion, and told me to take it for three weeks while keeping a journal of my symptoms (hair-related and otherwise), along with notes about anything that might be affecting me, like food or stress. I was to check in after those three weeks.

But the appointment wasn't over. I was in his office for another twenty minutes — double the time we'd spent discussing my hair — while he looked at my hands, feet, and back and asked questions about my skin. After that examination, he informed me in the most obnoxious tone that I had a large number of moles on my back and I was to call him immediately if I noticed any changes. He talked down to me the entire visit, just like he did his previous patients, and I was livid.

I swallowed that anger, and I followed his instructions diligently. I applied the thin, milky white lotion twice a day, every day, and put together a simple but effective tracker of days in the first column and symptoms across the next columns, followed by one for notes.

What the tracker turned up was surprising in its totality. The symptoms I wrote down in sequential order were bloating, constipation, burning scalp, insomnia, frequent urination at night, headaches, stress (ranging from low to high), tingling scalp, chest tension/asthma, irregular heartbeats, and diarrhea.

Clearly, I had been ignoring a lot of things for a long time.

I emailed the dermatologist's office for a follow-up appointment since nothing had changed with my hair. He wrote back that I should keep applying the lotion for three more weeks.

Nothing had changed by the end of the second three-week period. In fact, new bald spots had emerged and the pain in my scalp had intensified. On a scale of one out of 10 where 10 meant this pain would literally kill me, I was a nine after my last wash day. I'd been sending multiple follow-up emails to schedule a follow-up appointment which went unanswered, so having nothing to go on but my own deductive reasoning, I sent a final, terse email asking if I might be experiencing an allergic reaction to products and if he could provide me with a referral for testing. He

emailed a referral, but never offered to schedule that follow-up.

Well, I was done with that doctor. I didn't even act
on his referral. Instead, I made an appointment to see another dermatologist — a man of color, though not Black —
who was referred to me by a friend. The earliest I could get
an appointment with him was October, 10 months after I
saw the first two bald spots.

SHOCK

_____

The second dermatologist was part of a large practice, and his office was located in a somewhat modern three-story building. The waiting room was blue and calming, but the exam room was unsettling with its overly bright fluorescent lights, white tiled floors, and walls half covered with blue-painted wood paneling and half covered with a wallpaper consisting of a simple blue and red geometric pattern against a stark white background.

I had written down everything I wanted to share with the intention of communicating my story faster and more seamlessly this time. This doctor listened carefully and didn't interrupt me once. Afterwards, he went through my hair carefully and completely with his bare, sanitized hands, then shared that, from a clinical perspective, I might have three forms of alopecia going on all at once: alopecia areata, central centrifugal cicatricial alopecia (CCCA), and androgenic alopecia. His tone was sensitive, but he was talking fast and I couldn't process everything he was saying in real time. Nor was I able to conjure up a single question before my appointment ended with him electronically submitting three oral medications and a different topical steroid to my pharmacy and requesting that I schedule a follow-up appointment in three months at the check-out desk. He also shared that if things didn't improve by then, he would perform a scalp biopsy to obtain a definitive diagnosis.

That was a lot to take in — the news and all the drugs. I was terrified and sat in my car without moving for 10 minutes before I could calm myself enough to drive home.

A high degree of stress or fear makes me unequipped to respond in the moment, as I've already demonstrated. It took the entire one-hour drive back to Baltimore for me to calm down. When I relayed what happened to my husband, he advised that I not wait three months for a definitive diagnosis and, instead, call the doctor's office the next day. I did that and secured an appointment for a biopsy the following week.

The dermatologist took two, four-millimeter sections out of my scalp — one from the center front of my head, about an inch back from my hairline, and another about three inches back from that. The procedure didn't hurt because he injected me with a local anesthetic, although the sensation and sound of him cutting into my scalp was quite disconcerting. At the end of the procedure, I asked if it was safe for me to fly to the West Coast on Thursday for my best friend's father's funeral. He said I'd be fine provided I follow his instructions for keeping the wounds clean and take ibuprofen when I needed it.

By the next day, I could feel a new and different type of pain in the area of both sites. This, I expected. What I didn't expect was waking up on Thursday with swelling from the top of my forehead down to my right eye. I was intensely worried, and for this reason I canceled my early flight from the East Coast that morning because I thought I was having an allergic reaction and assumed I needed medical attention. I left an urgent message for the dermatologist, who called me as soon as he got it. By then it was too late for me to book a new flight that would have gotten me to the West Coast in time for the funeral. My best friend was completely understanding, still, I felt awful for not being there for her at a time of sudden grief.

For three weeks after the biopsies, my scalp felt like it was being stretched by a torture device, though it was just the pressure of the sutures holding my skin together while the scalp tissue fused and healed. It was hard for me to focus at work, it hurt to chew food, I struggled to exercise, and I couldn't sleep. On top of that, the tension caused a headache that lasted until the healing was complete. While I knew I needed those biopsies, I regretted subjecting my scalp to more torture.

The conclusion, drawn by the dermatopathologist who examined both specimens, was central centrifugal cicatricial alopecia — CCCA.

CCCA is a form of scarring alopecia that almost exclusively occurs in Black women over the age of 30.[14] It's estimated that CCCA may affect up to 15-percent of Black women (almost two million over age 30 in the U.S. alone),[15] though the precise number is unknown.[16] A Black woman dermatologist I later met with — who says she sees 20 CCCA patients a day — estimates the number is upwards of 25- or 30-percent, given the high occurrence in her practice. She just thinks many of us are walking around undiagnosed.

With scarring alopecia, an inflammatory process attacks the hair follicles. If the hair follicle is destroyed by that process, a scar forms underneath the surface of the scalp, which prevents hair from ever growing again. According to dermatologist Yolanda Lenzy, the hair loss from

---

[14] Aguh, Crystal, and Amy McMichael. "Central Centrifugal Cicatricial Alopecia." *JAMA Dermatology* 156, no. 9 (2020): 1036. https://doi.org/10.1001/jamadermatol.2020.1859.

[15] Calculated as 15% of Black women over age 30 as reported by census.gov. on January 28, 2024 at https://data.census.gov/table/ACSDT5YSPT2021.B01001?q=United+States&t=004&g=010XX00US.

[16] Aguh and McMichael, "Central Centrifugal Cicatricial Alopecia," 1036.

CCCA can be devastating, with some patients having up to 75-percent scarring on their scalps.[17]

Initially referred to as "hot comb alopecia"[18] in 1968, later as "follicular degeneration syndrome"[19] and "chemically induced alopecia,"[20] CCCA was believed to be caused by Black hair grooming practices. Yet, even women who've never used harsh hair care products or worn tight, tension-inducing hairstyles still develop CCCA."[21] A study in 2009 reported an association between weaves, cornrows, and braids with artificial hair extensions (i.e., scalp tension) and CCCA,[22] however, a direct link was and still is unclear.

More recently conducted research suggests that a genetic predisposition,[23] variants in gene expression (specifically, mutations in the gene that encodes an enzyme critical to hair shaft formation),[24] a disruption of the balance between proinflammatory and anti-inflammatory fac-

[17] DocSwiner, dir. *New Year New You 2021: Dr. Yolanda Lenzy's Interview*. 2021. 23:38. https://www.youtube.com/watch?v=AzPY3vjigRM.

[18] LoPresti, Philip, Christopher M. Papa, and Albert M. Kligman. "Hot Comb Alopecia." *Archives of Dermatology* 98, no. 3 (1968): 234–38. https://doi.org/10.1001/archderm.1968.01610150020003.

[19] Sperling, L. C., and P. Sau. "The Follicular Degeneration Syndrome in Black Patients. 'Hot Comb Alopecia' Revisited and Revised." *Archives of Dermatology* 128, no. 1 (1992): 68–74.

[20] Nicholson, A.G., C. C. Harland, R. H. Bull, P. S. Mortimer, and M. G. Cook. "Chemically Induced Cosmetic Alopecia." *British Journal of Dermatology* 128, no. 5 (1993): 537–41. https://doi.org/10.1111/j.1365-2133.1993.tb00231.x.

[21] Starks, Sierra Leone. "Why This Common Form of Hair Loss in Black Women Is Often Misdiagnosed." Allure, August 31, 2021. https://www.allure.com/story/central-centrifugal-cicatricial-alopecia.

[22] Gathers, Raechele Cochran, and Henry W. Lim. "Central Centrifugal Cicatricial Alopecia: Past, Present, and Future." *Journal of the American Academy of Dermatology* 60, no. 4 (2009): 660–68. https://doi.org/10.1016/j.jaad.2008.09.066.

[23] Dlova, Ncoza C., Francois H. Jordaan, Ofer Sarig, and Eli Sprecher. "Autosomal Dominant Inheritance of Central Centrifugal Cicatricial Alopecia in Black South Africans." *Journal of the American Academy of Dermatology* 70, no. 4 (2014): 679–682.e1. https://doi.org/10.1016/j.jaad.2013.11.035.

[24] Malki, Liron, Ofer Sarig, Maria-Teresa Romano, et al. "Variant PADI3 in Central Centrifugal Cicatricial Alopecia." *New England Journal of Medicine* 380, no. 9 (2019): 833–41. https://doi.org/10.1056/NEJMoa1816614.

tors,[25] and autoimmunity[26] are causes of CCCA. Scientists also say that CCCA becomes more likely to manifest if other conditions such as type 2 diabetes[27], uterine fibroids[28], and seborrheic dermatitis[29] are present.

Whatever the cause(s), I have it, and there's no known singular cause or course of treatment.

Across several visits, my second dermatologist prescribed multiple medications: baricitinib, oral minoxidil, finasteride, fluocinolone acetonide oil (a topical steroid in base of peanut oil) that stained my pillows, and later an alcohol-based liquid metformin solution that dried out my hair. I also had multiple rounds of steroid injections in my scalp in six to eight-week cycles. Being injected with a shot in the arm is a little painful, however, it's short and quick. Being injected in the scalp once, let alone twenty times, hurts far more. Even though the process took just over one minute, it was brutal to endure.

As all of this was unfolding, my stylist connected me with a client of hers who also has CCCA. When we spoke by phone, it was helpful to hear that she too experienced pain, which for her felt like being bitten by fire ants. I also

[25] Anzai, Alessandra, Eddy Hsi Chun Wang, Eunice Y Lee, Valeria Aoki, and Angela M Christiano. "Pathomechanisms of Immune-Mediated Alopecia." *International Immunology* 31, no. 7 (2019): 439–47. https://doi.org/10.1093/intimm/dxz039.

[26] Subash, Jacob, Tiffany Alexander, Victoria Beamer, and Amy McMichael. "A Proposed Mechanism for Central Centrifugal Cicatricial Alopecia." *Experimental Dermatology* 29, no. 2 (2020): 190–95. https://doi.org/10.1111/exd.13664.

[27] Kyei, Angela, Wilma Fowler Bergfeld, Melissa Piliang, and Pamela Summers. "Medical and Environmental Risk Factors for the Development of Central Centrifugal Cicatricial Alopecia: A Population Study." *Archives of Dermatology* 147, no. 8 (2011): 909–14. https://doi.org/10.1001/archdermatol.2011.66.

[28] Aguh, Crystal, Yemisi Dina, C. Conover Talbot, and Luis Garza. "Fibroproliferative Genes Are Preferentially Expressed in Central Centrifugal Cicatricial Alopecia." *Journal of the American Academy of Dermatology* 79, no. 5 (2018): 904-912.e1.

[29] Okwundu, Nwanneka, Chiagoziem Ogbonna, and Amy J. McMichael. "Seborrheic Dermatitis as a Potential Trigger of Central Centrifugal Cicatricial Alopecia: A Review of Literature." *Skin Appendage Disorders* 9, no. 1 (2023): 13–17. https://doi.org/10.1159/000526216.

appreciated learning what medication she was using — a steroid shampoo that my dermatologist never mentioned. This shampoo, along with monthly steroid shots, kept her from experiencing flares, so I decided to make an appointment with her doctor — a Black woman — in the hope that I could get down to fewer and more efficacious treatments.

When I called, I was lucky to land an appointment on her calendar during the small window in which she was accepting new patients.

After filling out my history online and sending her my biopsy results, I had a virtual consultation in April, six months after the confirmed CCCA diagnosis. Instead of removing medications she added even more to my treatment plan: "super high potency" clobetasol lotion to replace the "low potency" fluocinolone acetonide oil; a low dose of the antibiotic doxycycline; an ointment formulation of topical metformin to prevent scarring; and a dermaroller, a metal rolling device with sharp microneedles that I was to rub on my thinning and bald spots weekly to further prevent scarring. I tried the dermaroller but it hurt and it damaged my hair. Ultimately, I had to give it up because of a metal allergy soon to be revealed.

This third dermatologist told me if this collective of treatments didn't work, she'd add hydroxychloroquine — a medication for which one of the listed side effects is blindness — though she said she hadn't seen that occur with the low dosage prescribed for hair loss. If that didn't work, she said that platelet-rich plasma injections would be next, though insurance wouldn't cover any of the $650+ cost per session, which involved triple the number of scalp injections than the steroid shots. If that didn't work, she said there were additional therapies we could try. And if all of those treatments failed, tattooing could be a way of obscuring my bald spots.

I'm sure she intended all this as encouragement and hope for there being several options for keeping my hair, however, that is not how it landed with me at the time. I felt completely dejected and I was depressed for days. She also shared an important bit of information I hadn't heard before: I'd have to take medications for the rest of my life in order to keep the hair I still had.

PAIN

SENSATION

Pain is...*something*. It's debilitating. It's agonizing. It's maddening. It breeds confusion. It saps you of will and desire. Pain makes it difficult to sleep. To get through the day. To accomplish things. Pain stifles joy. Many times, I thought I might die. An entry in my personal journal read:

> *My head is on fire. This pain is going to kill me, or maybe I'll end up killing myself. I can't handle this. I'm not strong enough. I don't think I can exist in a body if I have to deal with this much pain.*

I first experienced pain in my scalp two months after noticing my first bald patches. It was a seething, burning, excruciating pain that would last for one to two weeks at a time, followed by a one- to two-day respite before flaring up again. The pain was particularly pronounced after I washed my hair. My scalp would turn a beet red color and it felt as though someone took dozens of hot sewing needles and stuck them in my head all at once. Maybe it's how a scalp would feel if it got stuck over and over with the sharp, fire-tinged edges of the woody base of the cotton boll.

The burning heat in my head would plague me, not for hours on end, but for days. The phrase "trial by fire" was constantly on my mind. Could CCCA be that for me?

Some sort of fucked up initiation to test my fortitude? But an initiation into *what*? I couldn't understand the divine lesson behind taking my hair and I especially didn't understand why I had to experience burdensome physical pain on top of deep emotional torment.

The truth is, I would certainly rather have no hair than excruciating pain.

On a scale of one to ten, the pain I experienced regularly ranged between seven and nine. None of the medications I was prescribed stopped the pain, so I was convinced I developed an allergy to something — especially since the pain became worse after hair washing. When I shared this at my first appointment with the second dermatologist, he said it "might" be possible but more likely it was neurological. He was hesitant to put me on an additional medication right away because he wanted to first see how I did with the other meds he prescribed. I agreed since I suspected an allergy was the issue and I asked how I could find out for sure. I was insistent enough that he referred me to an allergist for patch testing.

Because the allergist he recommended was booked for several months out, I opted for an appointment the very next day with another allergist in the same office. I was skeptical about seeing someone with an open schedule, but I couldn't afford to be choosy. I encouraged myself that I could and would get the answers I needed by repeating to myself: I am not powerless. I have a mind that's fully capable of reason. I have total control over my schedule and my time. I have access to resources. I can solve this problem once I have a plan that I can work.

Excursus

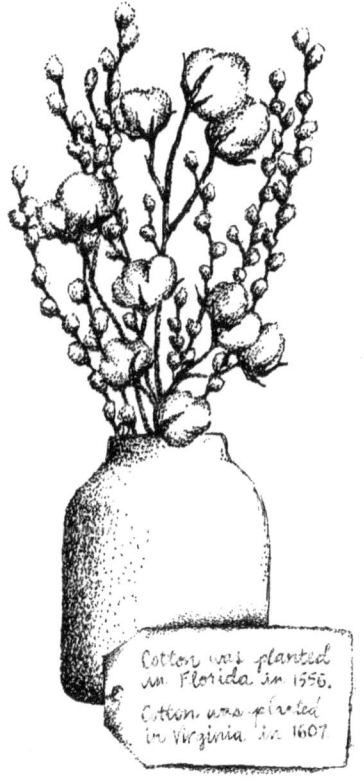

In 2020, I bought a cluster of cotton bolls, wrapped like you would fresh flowers, at a Juneteenth celebration. They were harvested by a Black farmer who intended them to be a symbol of liberation from bondage. The sign that came with the cluster, which I kept, reads, "Cotton was planted in Florida in 1556. Cotton was planted in Virginia in 1607."

This cluster of cotton sits in a vase interspersed among pussy willows in my living room. This vase will be one of the things I will take with me every place I live.

I've read narratives about how painful it is to pick cotton. I believe it because I stabbed my finger with a sharp end of a woody bit when I created this arrangement. The pain of being stuck by that boll is similar to the discomfort I feel in my scalp (minus the burning), making it an apt metaphor. Being pricked by cotton feels like a sudden, sharp sting that lingers after the initial injury. Cotton has hidden immune defenses, just like my scalp.

SOLUTIONING

I met with the allergist, an early 30s white woman, who said she'd perform an NAC-80 patch test. It's supposedly the "most comprehensive" allergen test in existence. She also told me I could bring additional products to test if there was anything I suspected I was allergic to that didn't appear on the list of 80 known allergens.

When I got home, I went through the list of what was covered by the test and barely saw any of the ingredients I recalled being listed as ingredients in my hair products. Because I was desperate and wanted definitive answers, I spent hours cataloging every single ingredient in every product that my stylist or I used in a spreadsheet — there were over 200 — then compared my list to what was covered by the patch test. The patch test covered just 20 of those ingredients. I emailed the allergist the results of my analysis, shared my concern that the patch test covered only a small percentage of the ingredients, and asked for confirmation of the maximum number of products I could bring. She emailed back this:

> "Hi...there are 2 issues with bringing and applying so many extra products
>
> 1. insurance (will only cover so much patch testing) and
>
> 2. surface area on your back! The 80 patches that are part of our testing fits most of your back, so really there is only room for a few extra patches.
>
> Many of the ingredients/chemicals we test for go by many different names. I wonder if some of the

ingredients you want tested for are actually included in the 80 but just a different name.

Lastly, we do not want to apply any products (like chemical straighteners, etc.) that could burn the skin (or not supposed to be on the skin for many days at a time)."

I laughed out loud at that last paragraph. Did she really think any Black woman would leave a chemical straightener on their skin for days? Also, could she not see that my hair was natural?

I let her know I would pay the extra cost for whatever insurance doesn't cover, told her my hair was chemical-free, and shared that I already reviewed every single product in the patch test against other names on the testing company's website, hence my conclusion that the gap between what the test covers and what is contained in my products was indeed very large. I then asked what my options would be for additional testing and her response was, "There is one dermatologist in DC who specializes in patch testing. You could potentially reach out to his office and see if they have any thoughts."

In other words, she had no clue.

I showed up for the patch testing with seven products in total; a shampoo and conditioner that I'd been using for over a decade, a new shampoo and conditioner from a "hair growth" product line, another new shampoo and conditioner formulated by a dermatologist for people with product sensitivities, and one styling product I'd been using for the past few months. It's worth noting that the new products I brought were the results of hours of online research into products with few ingredients and minimal overlap with the products I'd been using.

When I showed up for my appointment, my allergist — the one who earlier said that I could bring in products to test — told me they couldn't be applied because the patch testing wasn't appropriate for products you rinse off the skin after application. In fairness to her, she did state at a later date that I could apply "maybe about 5 extra products as long as they are safe to place on skin for 72 hours," but in my mind that didn't exclude shampoos and conditioners.

I was pissed and I let her know it. I told her she knew from the very beginning that I came to her office because I was in severe pain and desperate to find out what hair product ingredient(s) I might be allergic to. It seemed the impact of my words and/or tone made her give in because her assistant applied all the products I brought with me.

The patch test was a four-day process. Patches were applied to my back on a Monday and I was instructed not to bathe or shower until after my first reading, two days later on a Wednesday. That reading showed that none of the hair products had caused a reaction. The next day, Thursday, was the final reading and I was surprised by the results: I had zero reaction to the 20 ingredients that were in my hair products and I had zero reaction to my old shampoo, conditioner, and styling product, despite having an extremely irritated scalp after applying them. I did, however, have an allergic reaction to nickel, cobalt, and the "hair growth" shampoo, and an irritant reaction to methyl methacrylate, bacitracin, textile dye mix, and the dermatologist-formulated shampoo. None of this gave me an explanation for the scalp pain and I felt devastated. By this time, I hadn't washed my hair in four weeks and was still afraid to. I was at a loss for the next right step so I asked the doctor, and her response was, "I don't know."

Dejected, I circled back with my second dermatologist who made the referral to get his thoughts on what I should do next. Because my pain levels far exceeded those of his other CCCA patients, he concluded the pain was neurological (specifically, scalp dysesthesia) and prescribed a nerve pain medication called gabapentin. I later learned, from the Black woman dermatologist I'd been seeing alongside him, that lots of women with CCCA experience pain or itching or tenderness, which made me question if he really believed me or if his patient population was too small to be representative.

I don't know the answer. I do know that I doubted the sincerity of his belief in what I was saying and experiencing — a common reality for Black women, especially in medical settings, regardless of education or income level. Even someone as visible and accomplished as Serena Williams wasn't immune. After giving birth, she recognized the signs of a pulmonary embolism, a condition she had experienced before, and yet her concerns were initially dismissed. She had to insist on a CT scan and a heparin drip — interventions that ultimately saved her life.[30]

I wanted an end to the pain, yet I was concerned about being on several meds already and unsure whether gabapentin was the right next step. For this reason, I reached out to a friend who's a neurologist to see what he thought about that medication and its applicability to CCCA.

He was honest with me and said most neurologists aren't likely to have experience with CCCA, as he'd never

[30] Haskell, Rob. "Serena Williams on Motherhood, Marriage, and Making Her Comeback." Vogue, January 10, 2018. https://www.vogue.com/article/serena-williams-vogue-cover-interview-february-2018.

heard of it himself. In any case, he assured me that gabapentin is a safe drug and the dosage my doctor advised was on the very low side of what is typically prescribed. After our conversation, I began taking this new drug on top of the three oral medications I was already taking. Bottom line: after taking it for several weeks, gabapentin did nothing for me — not even after my dermatologist tripled the dosage.

To my surprise, and with deep appreciation, my friend went the extra mile and reached out to a dermatologist colleague, who then consulted with yet another specialist on my behalf. Here's what they shared with me:

> Dermatologist A (my neurologist-friend's colleague):
> "Yes, burning can be a symptom in CCCA. Gabapentin is a good idea. Simple things like topical steroids or steroid local injections might help. Also important: being really gentle with the hair and washing regularly but being careful to avoid hair shaft desiccation."

> Dermatologist B (the doctor his colleague consulted):
> "Totally agree. Specifically would a) confirm diagnosis and b) try other things like intralesional steroids first if inflammation is present OR, try cooling agents like menthol or peppermint oil if I suspect it's isolated scalp dysesthesia.

> In my clinic, I see scalp burning often presenting without accompanying hair loss and it is quite common. Therefore, it is possible for both to exist and not be related to each other."

These responses struck me as simultaneously helpful and not helpful.

After patch testing, adding in neurological medication, and having the benefit of two more dermatologists' perspectives, I was no closer to knowing the source of the pain.

I didn't know what else to do. I was at a loss. I tried all the options my doctors had given me and nothing lessened the pain. Nothing brought me relief. Not one thing. My dermatologist said he'd prescribe a stronger neurological medication, but I wasn't certain that this was neurological. I wasn't getting anywhere with my current doctors and, after 11 months of being in agonizing pain, I tried to make up for conventional medicine's structural failures and diagnostic blind spots by reaching out to a clinical herbalist I trusted for advice on next steps. I mentioned the idea of consulting with a functional medicine doctor in the hopes someone with that type of expertise could help me uncover and treat the underlying imbalance of the pain rather than chasing the symptom of pain. This herbalist agreed that seeing a functional medicine doctor made sense and he made some inquiries to identify someone for me. He gave me two names: I got no response from the first functional medicine doctor I called (twice), however, I did get a response from the second and I set up an appointment.

My first appointment with the functional medicine doctor was in January of 2023, 15 months after my CCCA diagnosis. Because he didn't take insurance, I paid $595 for that appointment, plus $330 for a lab test and $295 for my follow-up appointment scheduled for March, at which time we'd discuss the test results. The supplements he recommended cost almost $400 a month. Those supplements covered a lot of ground and helped me with fundamental issues like sleep, mood, and energy. The inflammation-modulating-specific supplements even slightly turned down the volume of the pain. Even so, disruptive pain persisted.

Nothing I'd done — not the steroid injections, the medications, nor the supplements — had taken away the pain.

I was convinced the pain was the "CCCA process" happening in real time — like my body was waging war on itself.

GUILT

———

Repeatedly, I'd wonder why this happened to me. If there was any truth to the theory that hair grooming practices caused CCCA, I was guilty. If seborrheic dermatitis is a contributing factor, I'm pretty sure I had it throughout my relaxed years and a bit beyond, yet I'd done nothing to treat it other than the occasional dandruff shampoo. If it's genetic, then I must have done something, maybe even thought something to go from having a genetic predisposition to full-blown gene expression. Maybe this was the result of a period of high mental stress compounded by the physical stress of major surgery that broke the camel's back. Or perhaps it was a combination of all of the above. I agonized over my responsibility. Over what I might have done or not done, thought or not thought, leading me to analyze every decision — and indecision — whose consequences might be my suffering.

Whatever the actual cause, I believed it was my fault somehow. Sometimes, I still do.

I blame myself for not having the courage to resist white supremacist beauty standards sooner in life. I blame myself for the damage I caused my hair and my scalp from intense heat and chemicals. I blame myself for not treating my hair with the care it deserves. Mostly, I feel guilty for all the negative thought patterns about my hair. For not loving, appreciating, and praising every single hair on my head no matter how kinky, how straight, or how my locs were formed. No matter how much my roots resisted taming in a relaxed or loc'd state. No matter how quickly my strands turned gray.

I don't "do" guilt generally because I believe in being a moral person and, therefore, saying and doing things that don't lead to regret. However, I do feel guilty about being afflicted with CCCA.

I feel guilty about losing my hair and the pain my body experiences. And I feel guilty, because I can't do anything to stop the process or relieve the pain, short of taking medications for life.

ANGER

———

I am angry that this is my fate and the fate of two million Black women in the U.S. alone. I am angry that after embracing my natural hair in my 30s, I'm losing it in my 50s in a manner that is slow and painful.

In 2010 I earned a master's of science degree in herbal medicine from an integrative health university in Maryland. My favorite teacher there once said he views physiology and pathophysiology as a metaphor for life. Those words have stuck with me and I challenge myself to name the metaphor whenever I experience a health issue or crisis.

Asthma, to use one example, results from hypersensitivity to one's environment. In the presence of commonplace elements such as mold, pollen, dust, smoke, chemicals, and animal dander, the immune system kicks off an inflammatory response and the bronchial tubes of the lungs constrict, which prevents air from moving easily in and out of the lungs. The consequence of that physiological response is you have to work harder to breathe.

I'm asthmatic. I'm also highly empathic and, therefore, hypersensitive to the emotional environment around me and what people are feeling. When people around me are stressed, I tend to take their stress atop of my own, which makes my relationships, especially those at work, harder to navigate. Asthma is my metaphor for porous emotional boundaries.

I know from the biopsies performed on my scalp

and the "horizontal sections" examined, that these things, barely decipherable to my mind, were detected:

Tissue sample #1: eccentric epithelial atrophy, follicular scars and follicular stellae, follicular miniaturization, and sparse perifollicular lymphocytic inflammation near the isthmus/infundibulum

Tissue sample #2: eccentric epithelial atrophy with perifollicular fibrosis and moderately dense lymphohistiocytic inflammation

In simple terms, I translate this as tissue deterioration, injury, and heat.

I believe CCCA is my life's metaphor for misogynoir. Its symptoms are the consequences of the trauma Black women experience that is often unseen.

I am angry at the microaggressions, aggressions, and injustices Black people face every day, no matter where in the world we live. And I'm angry because I will not see the end of anti-Blackness and misogynoir in my lifetime.

DESPERATION (→ CONFUSION)

————

Anger can be productive when it leads to action, so I channeled my anger into doing everything I could with the hope of preventing further hair loss, alleviating pain, and tempering my suicidal thoughts. I told myself that if I maintained the hair I still had, I could hide what I lost. As Zora Neale Hurston said, it was a "go hard or go home" kind of situation.[31]

NON-DERMATOLOGICAL PURSUITS

In addition to the conventional medicine path I was on, I tried every other modality I could think of to gain relief from pain. I saw a functional nutritionist, wellness consultant, trichologist, clinical herbalist, and acupuncturist. Acupuncture helped the most because it dialed the pain back considerably. But I still felt pain.

I also worked on my mind. I continued seeing my therapist, who is trained in cognitive behavior therapy and focuses on healing from racial trauma. I worked one-on-one with a holistic doctor who taught me a form of active meditation designed to heal the physical body by first healing the energetic body. I tried positive visualization. I even downloaded an app that educated me on somatic tracking and word swapping among other things. I made some progress with each of these mental modalities.

———

[31] Hurston, Zora Neale. *You Don't Know Us Negroes and Other Essays*. Edited by Henry Louis Gates Jr. and Gene Andrew Jarrett. New York: Library of America, 2022.

For example:

I could catch and halt a negative thought pattern, of which there were some deep and heavy ones:

I'll be ostracized for being bald.
I'll look funny bald because my head is misshapen.
My husband won't find me attractive without hair.

I used the Thought Record Sheet my therapist gave me to challenge myself on the validity of my negative thoughts and, sometimes, I could bring myself relief from my worst thoughts.

I could put myself into a meditative state to clear my energy and visualize turning down a volume knob to lower the pain. I could lean into the pain I was feeling in my scalp and explore the sensations of it from a place of mindfulness and detached curiosity to let my brain know I was safe. I even began using different language for pain to interrupt, instead of reinforce, the cycle:

My head doesn't feel as comfortable and cool as I'd like it to right now.
The animals in my mind's zoo are at it again with the shenanigans.

On days when I was feeling hopeful, I'd tell myself this is epigenetics and, if I did something to turn CCCA "on," maybe I could turn it off. But then the pain would return (albeit, somewhat lessened with my new mental practices) or I'd see more bald spots. As quickly as hope would come, it would go.

Before all this, I couldn't remember the last time I cried. This situation made me cry all the time, involuntarily. When the pain is at its worst, tears stream down my face without effort on my part. The muscles of my face don't move. My eyes don't squinch. The tears just flow like a steady river. I know tears are healing from an emotional standpoint and my meditation teacher, who is also an acupuncturist, told me they release cortisol too — which makes sense because I was seriously stressed out.

NOT CCCA?

When I was first diagnosed with CCCA, I had hoped to get an appointment with a Black woman dermatologist I'd researched whose office was closer to my home. Her first appointment for a new patient was one year out, thanks to a COVID pandemic-induced backlog. I booked it knowing I could always cancel it later.

I never did cancel that appointment, and when the time for it arrived, I met with this woman — a fourth dermatologist — anticipating she would confirm the course of action I was on for CCCA. I figured it would be validating and thus helpful because I still had doubts since I still had pain.

I traveled 30 minutes to my appointment to another run-of-the-mill doctor's office. She examined my hair and scalp while listening to me recap the history of my symptoms, past diagnoses, biopsy findings, and treatments.

Then she sat down across from me and said I did *not* have CCCA.

Upon hearing those words, I was shocked and bewildered. Given my typical "freeze" response to stress, I had no words at all for an entire minute, which must feel like an eternity in "doctor-time" because she ended my appointment before I could fully process her words.

When I got into my car, I replayed everything else she said in my mind.

She told me that biopsies in Black women aren't helpful because when they see "Black," they always say it's CCCA.

Her diagnosis was androgenic alopecia and scalp dysesthesia.

She said minoxidil is the best treatment for androgenic alopecia so I should continue that, but I should discontinue the baricitinib and steroid injections my other doctors had prescribed.

She then instructed me to continue taking the low-dose naltrexone that my integrative primary care physician prescribed at my most recent physical, keep seeing my acupuncturist, and apply hair products with peppermint oil and cold packs to my head to address the pain when it flares.

Lastly, she said I should come back in six months.

In my desperation to uncover any additional solution to the pain, I inadvertently ended up in a situation where I became utterly confused about what and who to believe, and therefore, what to do next. There is no way for me — a non-medical professional — to reconcile the different diagnoses I've received. And there's no way I could get these dermatologists and the dermatopathologist who wrote the biopsy report in a room together to reach a consensus, which meant I had to decide which dermatologist I trusted the most.

In the meantime, I sent photos of my scalp and my biopsy report to the fourth dermatologist asking for her explanation of the findings since she ruled out CCCA. She never responded to that request, nor the follow-up message I left. Nevertheless, I followed her advice and stopped taking the baricitinib because of wishful thinking and the fact that I didn't really want to be on it given its potential side effects. It took less than two weeks for me to reach pain levels of eight and nine, so I posited she was wrong about my not needing it and resumed the medication. When I wrote her a third message telling her that, she responded by dismissing me. This is what she wrote:

> "Fortunately, there is no visible redness in your scalp, from the pictures everything looks normal. It is possible that this is an issue with clarity from the pictures and is one of the reasons why we always recommend follow up appointments if you require evaluation. Your biopsy reports also do not change the discussion we had at length when we discussed that 4mm biopsies often fail to capture the bigger clinical impression."

I responded by giving her a bigger piece of my mind and that concluded our discussions.

A few weeks later, at the next appointment with my third dermatologist — the one I trusted the most because she took the pain most seriously — I shared everything that transpired with the fourth dermatologist and asked if another biopsy, this time using her lab, would turn up a more definitive diagnosis. She said we could do that "for peace of mind," and I knew she meant my mind because I didn't get the sense *she* thought it was necessary.

Even though I asked for the biopsy, when I returned home, this is what I journaled:

The thought of having another hole cut in my head which would require weeks of recovery feels overwhelming right now. I function well when I have clarity and I know that doubt obstructs my healing, but is clarity of diagnosis worth putting my body through another biopsy? If I go bald eventually, do I really want to see a third scar on my head? What's the likelihood the biopsy will reveal something other than CCCA anyway? I don't know what to do. I'm so confused.

The biopsy was scheduled for two weeks later and, in preparation for the procedure, my dermatologist told me I'd need to be off baricitinib for one week prior. I started immediately, and by day five the volume of pain dialed back up to a continuous seven. My head felt like it was on fire and my scalp was red all over. Clearly, putting myself through the pain of another biopsy was unnecessary because I got a loud-ass, undeniable answer from my body about what to do, twice: Stop second guessing everything and take the baricitinib because this medication is what's keeping the pain from flaring and me from death's door.

I canceled that biopsy appointment.

When I told my meditation teacher about the conflicting diagnoses and the confusion I felt, here's what she said: "Your actual experience and symptoms are always the truth, and everything else is just a label." I appreciated that, though perhaps not as fully as I should have because my mind still wanted a definitive answer.

So I requested a second read of my original biopsy slides by my third dermatologist's dermatopathologist — who she said is one of the best in the country — and he concluded that the specimen from the front of my head was traction alopecia and the second was late stage CCCA.

The traction alopecia diagnosis was unexpected, but at least I could wholly acknowledge CCCA, appreciate that there was nothing more to be learned, and allow myself to accept what is.

COMPASSION

———

My emotions about pain and hair loss would shift from one day to the next, sometimes from one hour to the next. I'd cycle between anxiety, bitterness, fright, frustration, indignation, remorse, panic, resentment, shame, sorrow, and stress. Not one of these emotional states served my highest good, yet this is the truth of my experience.

I've heard people talk about a "dark night of the soul," so I wasn't unfamiliar with the term when my meditation teacher used it to describe this period of hair loss and pain.[32] After reading more about it, I understand it to mean a period of intense difficulty, disruption, or anguish that a person must experience in order to break down the ego, learn spiritual lessons, awaken to profound truths, or transform spiritually before reaching a higher vibrational existence.

To call this period of pain and hair loss a "dark night of the soul" seems appropriate. And if I processed everything I read correctly, it seems the only way to get past it is to go through it. But going through it — as members of my care team have told me — requires that I have compassion for myself, albeit unnatural to me because of outdated beliefs about deservedness and worthiness.

In the midst of a particularly bad pain episode when I couldn't eat, sleep, or move, I made a decision: I would gift myself compassion every day, especially when I was struggling with pain, guilt, anger, and/or desperation.

---

[32] "Dark night of the soul" refers to an untitled, eight-stanza poem of five lines each, written by San Juan de la Cruz in the 16th century when he was imprisoned for being a Catholic friar.

" "

Never be limited by other people's limited imaginations.

- Dr. Mae Jemison

PART III

FINDING GRACE AND HEALING

REVELATIONS

———

HAIR

"True liberation of my hair came when I stopped trying to control it in any state and just accepted it as it is."

— bell hooks, "Straightening Our Hair"

I was nine months into my CCCA diagnosis before I accepted the inevitability of total or near-total hair loss. Perhaps that is the gift pain gave me because I'd rather have no hair than be in pain. But the process is slow. Even if I did nothing, it would be years, perhaps decades before it's over and my scalp becomes a barren cotton field.

I thought a lot about my hair over these many months and this is perhaps my most profound learning: My uncooperative roots were always a message. My roots were doing their best to free my mind from white supremacist beauty standards and let my body show its natural beauty to the world. Even when my mind resisted, my body showed up every day, not in protest, but in love.

The fact is: **Black hair is extraordinary.** *My* **hair is extraordinary.**

First, our hair has the most texture, which means we can style, shape, and sculpt our hair in any way we choose. No other ethnicity of people can do with their hair what we Black people can naturally do with ours. Black people are natural-born designers and builders of great works of art that sit atop our heads.

Second, our hair stays clean the longest. My use of the word "clean" is purposeful. The natural oils produced by sebaceous glands don't travel down tightly coiled Black hair at the fast rate it does people with no coils, which means we don't need to wash our hair at the same frequency for it to stay healthy. And that means we can rock a fro, locs, weaves, braids, and all kinds of other styles for one week, two weeks, three weeks, four weeks — whatever is right for our texture and in line with our personal preferences and style of the moment. I reject all programming and belief systems that espouse Black people are "dirty" or "nasty" because we don't wash our hair every day.

I believe there are two reasons why our hair has been misperceived, ridiculed, policed, and criminalized: fear and envy. Fear and envy of our beauty are the reasons Tignon Laws were instituted in Louisiana in 1786 to mandate Creole women cover their hair, less they compete too freely with white women for status and the affection of white men.[33] Fear and envy of our hair's extraordinariness are the reasons why schools, companies, and government institutions (the U.S. military, for example) impose dress codes restricting how we can wear our hair — especially our natural hair. Fear and envy are what inspire the rampant appropriation by white people of our hairstyles.

I no longer allow discrimination against Black hair to go unchecked. I don't allow anyone to make Black women, Black men, Black nonbinary folk, or Black children feel self-conscious, embarrassed by, or ashamed of the hair on their heads while in my presence. In my presence, Black

---

[33] Gould, Virginia Meacham. "'A Chaos of Iniquity and Discord' Slave and Free Women of Color in the Spanish Ports of New Orleans, Mobile, and Pensacola." In *The Devil's Lane: Sex and Race in the Early South*, edited by Catherine Clinton and Michele Gillespie. Oxford University Press, 1997. https://doi.org/10.1093/acprof:oso/9780195112436.003.0016.

people will know themselves as beautiful humans with magnificently unique and beautiful hair.

But let us remember the words of the husband to the Black, bold, beautiful, bald, and badass Massachusetts Congresswoman, Ayanna Pressley: You don't need hair to wear a crown.

BODY

"And I said to my body, softly, 'I want to be your friend.' It took a long breath. And replied, 'I have been waiting my whole life for this.'"

— Nayyirah Waheed, "Three"

When I think about how I've treated my body over my lifetime, mostly I've thought of it as a tool of my mind. My mind would decide to have that cup of coffee, nevermind it increased my heart rate. My mind would decide to do full push-ups, despite the tenderness and discomfort in my shoulders the day after. My mind would agree to projects I knew would be stressful, ignoring the annoying mouth twitches I'd experience while working on the proposals and contracts.

I understand now that **the body is the place where the deepest wisdom and truth resides.** My body is constantly giving me subtle cues and messages when something is or isn't right for me. It's when I don't listen that what is subtle becomes obvious, that discomfort turns into disruption, that what is subclinical morphs or evolves into clinical diagnosis. That's when mouth twitches turn into horrible TMD (temporomandibular joint dysfunction), shoulder pain turns into rotator cuff tendonitis, and sustained, increased heart rate turns into premature ventricular contractions.

Unlike the examples related to my jaws, shoulder, and heart, with CCCA I can't name an obvious and straightforward path from subtle sign to full-blown disease, because the root cause was massive: a lifetime of trauma.

REST

———

"You were not just born to center your entire existence on work and labor. You were born to heal, to grow, to be of service to yourself and community, to practice, to experiment, to create, to have space, to dream, and to connect."

— Tricia Hersey, *Rest Is Resistance: A Manifesto*

I realize now that the only way my mind would permit my body to rest was to force me to recognize the signs of my internalized racial trauma, anger, and stress, then bring my mind to reckon with the pain it was causing. For myself and the Black women I know intimately, rest is something we're conditioned to not do. We often can't take a break (or we won't) out of fear others will think we're lazy. Self-care for many of us is a luxury we don't or can't afford ourselves. We rest only when we sleep well and maybe when we take vacations — *if* we ever permit ourselves a vacation.

I've overworked myself since childhood because I internalized what my parents and other people who love me told me: for Black people to get ahead we have to work three times as hard to get half as far.

Whether it was school or work, I'd spend way more time than I needed on a task because it couldn't just be "good enough," it had to be "perfect." I'd rewrite my homework when I was in grade school so there wouldn't be any crossed out words or mistakes. Preparing for a 15-minute presentation might take me 15 hours because every word had to be scripted, then rehearsed at least seven times — not because I didn't know the material, but because I was concerned I'd leave something out due to nerves or my speaking wouldn't be perfectly linear and fluent. I've pulled countless all-nighters, even into my 50s (when rebounding the next day isn't as easy), because of this belief system that "good enough" isn't enough when you're Black.

Racism does a number on us in numerous ways. The belief that we must grind constantly because of our responsibilities or how we might be perceived is another example, and this grinding comes at a heavy price to our physical and mental health.

My body had a lot of ways it tried to communicate that it needed rest and that I should slow down, yet I never listened until this health crisis came and I had no choice.

I've connected the dots over time and know my pain was most intense when my stress levels were high. That includes the stress of grinding myself to the bone at work and the stress of witnessing injustice after injustice directed toward Black bodies play out in the news and in real life. The pain wrought by CCCA was my body's cry for me to engage in productive rest. It should be the right of every human to have productive rest — time off from work, time away from the demands of family, time for quiet reflection, time for dreaming, time for creating — but many of us don't have, or think we don't have, the option of resting. That is, until our bodies force the issue.

I made a promise to myself once I understood that the intensity of the pain I experience correlates to my stress intensity: I will engage in productive rest every day. That could be eating breakfast and lunch away from my desk, taking 15-minute breaks throughout the workday, watching something fun on television, practicing modern calligraphy, reading a novel in the evenings before bed, or anything else that feels like it would serve my highest good. Every single day.

GIFTS

———

"If you surrender to the air, you could ride it."

— Toni Morrison, *Song of Solomon*

On one of my worst days, when the pain was at a nine out of 10, I couldn't do anything. I couldn't eat. I couldn't sleep. I couldn't work. I couldn't read. I couldn't talk. I couldn't move. All I could do was sit on my couch staring into a black TV screen with tears involuntarily streaming down my face as a form of release. I sat there with my feet on the floor and back against a thick pillow without moving for two or three hours. Then, out of the blue, I grabbed my cell phone, searched online for a mushroom illustration — because I'd been thinking about magic mushrooms and whether they could help shift my low spirits — grabbed my notebook, a pen, and some old colored pencils, and drew that mushroom.

I've wanted to draw my whole life but never thought I could. In grade school, I couldn't get the hang of animated stick figures. Not in a million years did I think I could draw something. The closest I got to art-making was learning modern calligraphy through an online course.

But on that day, in an episode of intense pain, I drew something.

And I kept finding images online to draw in my notebook: cotton, flowers, a fish, an octopus, and more.

I enjoy stippling the most — even though it's tedious and requires patience; a trait I didn't think I possessed. I can't be patient enough to peel a label off a jar without ripping it, yet somehow, I can sit for hours and make thousands and thousands of tiny dots on a page when I'm in intense pain. It's rewarding to finish a drawing and see how all those tiny dots come together to create beautiful shadows and texture. Those dots are gifts. They remind me of hair follicles and needles. And the ease and softness I feel when drawing remind me of the beautiful facets of cotton.

HEAT

**"To be a Negro in this country and to be
relatively conscious, is to be in a state of rage
almost all of the time."**

— James Baldwin, "The Negro in American Culture"

For me, CCCA is an intense heat that's too much for the
body to hold yet the body can't efficiently release it.
Instead, it burns off through painfully slow, excruciating
hair loss.

My acupuncturist said the words "Heart heat" at
my first appointment — six months into my CCCA diagnosis. I remember the immediate recognition and curiosity I
felt when she said it as I sat across from her in a window-lit
room with paintings that housed hidden spiritual messages
on three of the four walls and soothing instrumental music
playing in the background of the private treatment room. I
can't possibly recap what she said in a way that is precise,
complete, and wholly accurate, but I believe she said the
"Heart" — not the anatomical organ itself, rather the organ
system — sends heat it can't release to a part of the body
it deems safe, meaning a place where the heat will do the
least damage. My scalp was the third place my Heart sent
excess heat because the first place, my lungs, are too weak
to contain it because of asthma, and a hysterectomy freed
me of the second: fibroids. My mind was blown.

Acupuncture has been helpful in lessening pain
since the very early days of my treatments. Thankfully, my

health insurance covers them. I've experienced a level of relief and overall ease that conventional medicine wasn't and
isn't, it seems, able to provide.[34] After my first acupuncture
appointment, I was pain-free for two days straight. A week
later I had my second appointment and was pain-free until
the following week's appointment. After my third appointment, I was pain-free most of the time, with the pain only
reaching a level two at worst. After my fourth appointment,
when I did experience pain again, it stayed below a four.

Fast forward a couple of months, and I was mostly
at an occasionally-zero-but-mostly-low level of pain. That
was about nine months after my initial CCCA diagnosis.
Though there were moments and sometimes weeks of pain
spikes, I wasn't attached to acupuncture as the end-all be-
all solution, though I welcome it alongside all healing modalities that can bring me relief. At the very least, I now
have a framework for examining my thoughts and experiences.

I think about heat in a metaphorical sense now
and I can name what my heat is and where it primarily
comes from: anger.

Anger at myself for not appreciating and loving my
natural hair exactly as it is. Anger at a world that constantly
screams the message that Blackness is ugly and whiteness
is beautiful. And anger over the legion of microaggressions
and overt aggression I've experienced and witnessed over
Black hair, though my anger goes far beyond hair.

---

[34] While I credit acupuncture with alleviating the pain, I am and will always be a
huge fan of conventional medicine. I would never want to be without access to the
pharmaceutical medicine and treatments that have been lifesaving for me in other
ways. I simply acknowledge that conventional medicine has its limitations in the same
way traditional forms of medicine do. For me it's not an either/or but a both/and.

I'm angry about all the ways the U.S. and this world are fucked up. Not just in terms of racism and anti-Blackness, but sexism, misogyny, homophobia, transphobia, xenophobia, wealth inequality, poverty, war, climate change, and on and on. There's so much I'm angry about that I am full of heat. I am Heart-broken.

But I'm not without hope.

In the macro sense, I have hope that we can collectively repair the damage we've done. And, while I have detached from needing to hold onto the hair I have left, in the micro sense I have hope that I can minimize the pain of CCCA by finding ways beyond acupuncture needles to release the heat from my body, now that I know where it comes from and what it does.

(SELF)LOVE

"The moment we choose to love, we begin to move against domination, against oppression. The moment we choose to love we begin to move towards freedom, to act in ways that liberate ourselves and others. The action is the testimony of love as the practice of freedom."

— bell hooks, "Love as the Practice of Freedom"

Black women have big hearts and big hearts are easily damaged, especially by cruelty. It's a testament to our strength and resilience that we continue to love fiercely in the face of cruelty. Though, I believe that cruelty takes its toll in the form of high blood pressure, heart disease, fibroids, CCCA, and other conditions when we don't have the resources, tools, and methods to cope with our individual and collective Heart-brokenness.

I'm a Black woman with a big heart and the greatest challenges CCCA has brought into my life are learning to love myself fully and allowing my heart to remain open — regardless of whatever bad things occur in my life and irrespective of whether other people are open to receiving me as I am. To keep loving myself and to keep shining and radiating in the face of cruelty is not easy, especially the older I get because *shit*, I'm tired! But now I understand that withholding my radiance only damages me.

For the first time in my life, I can honestly say that I'm in the best relationship with my hair that I've ever been.

I give my hair permission to swell and lay exactly how it wants to — roots and all — and I genuinely love what I see when I look in the mirror. The irony is not lost on me that it took a painful disease to bring me into a more loving and satisfying relationship with my hair and, in that way, I'm grateful for CCCA. Grateful for its pain and the guilt, anger, and desperation I had to overcome in order to cultivate more compassion and love for myself and others.

To love is to offer healing, which makes Black women natural healers. We don't have to put forth effort to show up that way. Just being in our presence is healing. This is true of my mother, grandmother, aunts, cousins, colleagues and friends, and even Black women strangers I've met.

Black women, especially Black trans women, know what it's like to be *caste* down to the bottom and what that does to our bodies and our psyches. That's why we cultivate the capacity to love and see the value in everyone — regardless of outward appearance. At least, that's the case when we aren't operating from a place of white supremacy or of fear and insecurity, which includes succumbing to organized religion's tendency to reject and oppress. Absent the shackles of a white cis hetero patriarchy, to see and love everyone is our gift.

It is *my* gift.

This journey of hair loss has cleared the path for understanding how I can radiate my light and love in bigger ways. In keeping with many Black women I admire, I choose the expansiveness of love, for it serves my highest good and the highest good of everyone around me.

GRACE

——

**"She told them that the only grace they could have
was the grace they could imagine."**
— Toni Morrison, *Beloved*

I'm not a religious person, though I do adopt teachings
and pearls of wisdom from multiple traditions and spiritual practices because, though there are shadow sides to
organized religion, there's also light. From my take-what-
works-and-leave-the-rest approach to spirituality, it feels
right to conclude this book the way I started: with prayer.

If you are a Black woman experiencing hair loss,
may this book serve you in realizing you are not alone in
your questioning, emotions, and potentially the physical
pain the hair loss process might bring. May it aid you in
reflecting on your relationship to your hair and the experiences surrounding it, and may the insights and wisdom
that surface serve your health and well-being in the highest
and best ways.

If you are a Black woman with your hair intact,
may this book aid you in reflecting on your relationship
to your hair and the experiences surrounding it. And may
it elevate your love, appreciation, and regard for your hair
and the hair of the children in your life in the highest and
best ways.

If you are a Black man, may this book help you
understand the challenges of this journey, so you can be a

non-judgmental and loving resource to the Black women in your life — especially those experiencing hair loss.

If you're not Black, may you come to understand just how deep and insidious racism and anti-Blackness are and cease further perpetuating it with misconceptions, judgments, and offenses. And may you stand against the discrimination of Black hair and Black bodies, and advocate for our right to wear our hair natural — however we choose, wherever we choose.

And may we all be:

1. **Safe** to be who we are and take up space.

2. **Free** to be creative in the way we show up in the world.

3. **Strong** in our power to speed up and slow down in accordance with our bodies' needs.

4. **Compassionate** and loving toward others and ourselves.

5. **Clear** in mind, body, and spirit to speak our truths.

6. **In tune** with our bodies and guided by our bodies' innate wisdom.

7. **Aligned** to the highest version of ourselves.

ACKNOWLEDGMENTS

—

❝ ❞

**Let gratitude be the pillow upon which
you kneel to say your nightly prayer.**

- Maya Angelou, *Wouldn't Take Nothing for My Journey Now*

First and foremost, I give the greatest thanks to my husband, David: We married young when our lives were easy by comparison and I loved you then. Life has taken its toll as stress, exhaustion, and an accumulation of "paper cuts" turned into maladies, yet my love for you now is exponentially greater. You've been steadily by my side as I've evolved over the years. You've been my best teacher in learning to call beliefs into question. And you've loved me gently, fiercely, and in every other way I needed you to. It's the big things you do, like being my #1 champion and protector, and the little things, like bringing me breakfast in bed every morning and oiling my scalp with coconut oil and aloe vera gel when the pain starts, that make me count my lucky stars every day that we are here on Earth at this time for one another.

My brother, David: You are a beautiful human and a model sibling. I consider it a divine gift that I got to navigate childhood with you. And now that we are middle-aged — the years when adulthood feels especially burdensome and hard — I know I can count on your steadfast love and your continuous encouragement to face my fears and be the very best version of myself. That running joke about being stranded in the ocean? The truth is deeper: I believe I could achieve the impossible, the miraculous for you. And I know you could and would do the same for me.

Mom: I must pay special tribute to you for always doing the very best you could by me and for me. Raising children is no small feat and it's often thankless. I honor and cherish you for your unwavering love and for teaching me how to be and how not to be.

To each of my dear sister-loves, Karen, Nitza, and Yesenia: Your friendship is a whole world. It is comfort, joy, nourishment, authenticity, intelligence, humor, wit, candor, solace, celebration, healing, possibility...all the things. You enrich my life in countless ways and allow me the gift of being in a friendship where I can just sit back and receive when that's what I need. If you receive just a fraction of that enrichment in return from me, then know you are loved beyond measure.

Because this journey is personal and tells only my side of the encounters I've had, I chose not to associate experiences or words with specific people. At the same time, I want to acknowledge and thank my acupuncturist, therapist, meditation teacher, second and third dermatologists, clinical herbalist, Ayurvedic practitioner, Vedic counselor, functional nutritionist, primary care physician, functional medicine doctor, wellness consultant, stylists, and barber for their good care and support: You have all done right by me. I hope you recognize your "word medicine" within these pages.

To the many other friends and colleagues who've supported me in consistent or extraordinary ways — Aleksey, Alfredo, Ber-Henda, Doug, Elizabeth, James, Jeremy, Justin, Kyoko, Nissa, Pam, Rebecca, Sara, Shamire, and Stef: I treasure each and every one of you.

Ellen of ESaidSheSaid Communications: How grateful I am that the *Black Joy* newsletter led me to you. Talk about serendipity. I knew this book needed an editor before I shopped it, and you did that job beautifully. More than that: You encouraged me, validated me, and challenged me; gave me perspective and insights about publishing, networking, and life-ing that were worth more than gold; and brought joy and enthusiasm to our every conversation. You are a bright light.

Angel, of Silent Books Publishing: You are the personification of #blackgirlmagic. Your enthusiasm for my entire project (for there's more to come), thoughtful read of this book, encouragement to do more to "set the scene" and "create a deeper connection" with the reader, and partnership on every stage of the process far exceeded my expectations of the self-publishing experience. I am grateful for you and proud to be one of your Charm City authors.

Jess, how lucky am I that you were the artist to take on this project. You're a brilliant visual storyteller, and you knocked the cover image and design of this book out of the park. For as much as I love what you created, I value your understanding of my journey even more. That you read my entire manuscript, recognized the extra layers Black women have to navigate when it comes to beauty standards, felt the pain, sadness, and hope within your own body, and walked away changed is far beyond what I could have anticipated from our partnership.

Lastly, Congresswoman Ayanna Pressley from the state of Massachusetts, thank you for continuously modeling how to walk the journey of hair loss with grace.

MENTAL HEALTH RESOURCES

———

If parts of this story brought up hard emotions, please know that help is available. You don't have to face painful thoughts or feelings alone, for there are people ready to listen and help. Here are resources that may be available to you in and outside of the U.S.

IN THE UNITED STATES

If You're in Immediate Danger

- **Call 911** or go to your **nearest emergency room.** Many hospitals have mental health clinicians available who can offer immediate care and connect you to ongoing support.

If You're Thinking About Harming Yourself

- 988 Suicide and Crisis Lifeline - Call or **text 988**, or chat at **988lifeline.org**. Free, confidential, and available 24/7.

- Crisis Text Line - **Text HOME to 741741** to connect with a counselor by text message, any time of day or night.

- 2-1-1 - **Dial 211** to find local resources for counseling, social services, and community resources. This service is available in many states.

If You're Worried About Someone Else

- **Call 911** and **request a welfare check**, or call or text 988 Lifeline or chat at 988lifeline.org to receive guidance on how to help.

Other Helpful U.S. Resources

- National Alliance on Mental Illness (NAMI) HelpLine - Call **1-800-950-NAMI** (6264) or visit **nami.org/help**.

- Substance Abuse and Mental Health Services Administration (SAMHSA) Treatment Locator – Call **1-800-662-HELP** (4357) or visit **findtreatment.gov**.

OUTSIDE THE UNITED STATES

- Find a Helpline – Visit **findahelpline.com** for a global directory of crisis hotlines.

- Befrienders Worldwide – Visit **befrienders.org** for listening and emotional support services in many parts of the world.

- Samaritans (UK & Ireland): **Call 116 123** or visit **samaritans.org**.

DISCLAIMER

The resources listed here are for informational purposes only and do not constitute medical, psychological, or legal advice. The author assumes no responsibility for the accuracy, availability, or use of the resources, or for any actions taken based on this information and their outcomes.

A PHOTOGRAPHIC JOURNEY

Two twists

Graduation fancy

College/internship years

TWA #1, with texturizer

First loc extensions

My roots as they always
wanted to be

My locs, no extensions

Shaved sides

Second loc extensions

TWA #2

Face swelling post-biopsy

Hair lost in the crown

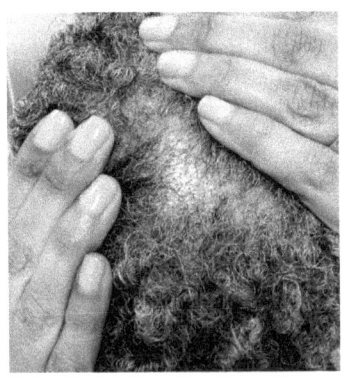

Scarred scalp (the shiny parts)

At peace with what is

ABOUT THE AUTHOR

Maya L. Johnson is a writer, entrepreneur, and advocate for Black women's health whose personal journey with central centrifugal cicatricial alopecia (CCCA) transformed the way she approaches beauty, self-worth, and healing.

After lifelong struggles with accepting her natural hair and later the shocking discovery of her own hair loss, Maya began exploring the deeper layers of identity, trauma, and resilience tied to Black hair.

Her memoir chronicles that transformation – from pain and fear to acceptance and empowerment – while amplifying the voices of millions of Black women navigating similar paths.

Through her online platform, CCCA Chronicles, she shares stories, insights, and resources to remind others that they are not alone on the journey toward self-acceptance, healing, and wholeness.

www.ingramcontent.com/pod-product-compliance
Lightning Source LLC
Chambersburg PA
CBHW051632120626
46551CB00014B/2044